Angelfishes of the World

by Kiyoshi Endoh

Book Design by Daniel N. Ramirez

Published by Ricordea Publishing
Miami Gardens, Florida 33169 USA

Oceanographic Series™

Angelfishes of the World
by Kiyoshi Endo

First Printing July 2007
10 9 8 7 6 5 4 3 2 1

Published and distributed by Two Little Fishies, Inc.
d.b.a. Ricordea Publishing
1007 Park Centre Blvd.
Miami Gardens, FL 33169 USA

Printed and bound by Mondadori Printing, Verona, Italy
Design and production by Daniel N. Ramirez
Translation by Tetsuo Otake
Edited by Julian Sprung
Photographs by Kiyoshi Endoh and others, as noted.

ISBN 10: 1-883693-26-8
ISBN 13: 978-1-883693-26-8

Table of Contents

The representative marine angelfish *Pomacanthus imperator* has a wide range from The Red Sea and Indian Ocean to the Pacific Ocean. The size of adults is over 30cm, and the colorful large body is remarkable to see on reefs. P/T. Nakamura (volvox)

Holacanthus africanus lives at the Cape Verde Islands in West Africa. P/T. Nakamura (volvox)

Angelfish look heavenly and are among the most remarkable of the colorful creatures found on coral reefs. They swim boldly and fearlessly sometimes, or weave through corals in an elegant way. The swimming style furthermore makes their color stand out. We instinctively respond to such flashy movement, and while most fishes simply escape at the sight of divers, angelfishes often stay, turn, and look back. In this moment a connection is made. Their manner seems to reveal their intellect. Whether by SCUBA diving or by having an aquarium we can meet and get to know these curious and beautiful creatures.

Keeping a marine aquarium is another way to get to know angelfishes. Many show the same charm in aquariums that they exhibit in nature, and most angelfish species easily become accustomed to captivity. The body coloration of juveniles and adults is often completely different, and in aquariums one can observe the growth and change over time. *Pomacanthus* and *Holacanthus* species grow to 25 to 60cm with color change phases, and they may live for more than two decades. In the entire group, the genus *Centropyge* is one of the best choices to keep in an aquarium. Just a 60L aquarium can make a habitat for long term keeping of *Centropyge* spp.

The famous freshwater angelfishes from the Amazon River in Brazil are not closely related to marine angelfishes.

The beautifully patterned *Centropyge potteri* is one of the pygmy angelfishes occurring in Hawaii & Midway.

Angelfishes mainly occur on coral reefs, but some of them occur on rock reefs at great depths or in the temperate zone. In Japan, diving points for observing them occur in regions as far north as Chiba. *Centropyge interrupta* and *Chaetodontoplus septentrionalis* adapt to the temperate zone, and diving at Izu Peninsula or South Ki Peninsula one can see these species. *Pomacanthus imperator, P. semicirculatus, Genicanthus lamarck, Centropyge heraldi,* and *C. tibicen* are observed at other places where the temperature remains above 20 °C.

Of course, it is better to have a larger tank for making a close-to-nature system. A large tank also has an advantage because it is easier to maintain stable water conditions. In this book, I introduce the charming points of angelfishes, with a main focus being their characteristics in aquariums. Angelfishes of the world are very diverse and mysterious. I hope you can find your favorite one in this book.

Food Habits

The mouth in angelfishes is small, and specialized to eat sponges, seaweeds, and plankton. The food preferences differ a little depending on the species, but most angelfishes are omnivorous. Both jaws have fine brush-like teeth to pick foods. Angelfishes cannot eat a lot at once, so they are always looking for food. They are not naturally fish eaters, but when housed in an aquarium with predators such as triggerfish and grouper, larger individuals of *Pomacanthus* spp. may adapt to compete for and eat small fishes offered as food to the predators.

Beautiful body color changing

Angelfish and butterflyfish, with their cute swimming style and well-designed body color and patterns, symbolize coral reef fishes. These characteristics make it easy for them to find each other. The colors and patterns are unforgettable, they bring joy to aquarists and divers, and books are made more vivid by them.

Sex changing, harems, and other reproductive strategies

Angelfishes change sex. Juveniles are females, and an individual with a large body becomes a male. The different types of angelfishes have different group habits. The group is a harem containing one male and several females in *Genicanthus* and many *Centropyge* species, while *Pomacanthus* species make a pair. Angelfishes are not a migratory, but have a territory. These habits help to spread their territories across coral reefs in shallow water to rock reefs in deep water.

The mouth of *Holacanthus ciliaris* is relatively small compared with the body. It is used to pick sponges from rocks.

Centropyge aurantonota and *Holacanthus tricolor* from the Caribbean have unique body colors and color patterns. These two are remarkable even though they reside in a home aquarium.

Genicanthus spp. have different colors in male and female, and they swim with great agility and speed. These characteristics distinguish them from other angelfishes.

6

Chaetodontoplus conspicillatus wears a mask, and the unique face makes her very popular with aquarists.
P/T. Nakamura (volvox)

Holacanthus passer cleaning the skin of a hammerhead shark. The adults of this species have a habit of forming large schooling groups.
P/T. Nakamura (volvox)

World Map of Angelfishes

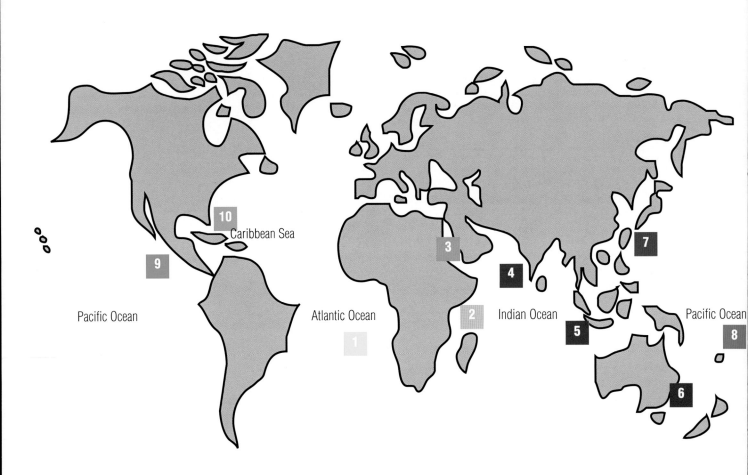

Caribbean Sea

Pacific Ocean

Atlantic Ocean

Indian Ocean

Pacific Ocean

Resplendent Pygmy Angelfish
Centropyge resplendens

Yellowbar Angelfish
Pomacanthus maculosus

Arabian Angelfish
Pomacanthus asfur

Regal Angelfish
Pygoplites diacanthus

Cocos Pygmy Angelfish
Centropyge joculator

Conspicuous Angelfish
Chaetodontoplus conspicillatus

Bluestriped Angelfish
Chaetodontoplus septentrionalis

Flame Angelfish
Centropyge loricula

Clarion Angelfish
Holacanthus clarionensis

Rock beauty
Holacanthus tricolor

Some people think that the ocean is just one big body of water around the world and the fish are the same everywhere in the Ocean, but of course that is not true. Currents, land masses, deep trenches, and difference of water temperature divide the ocean regions. Each area has a unique environment, and fishes in the area adapt in the environment to survive. Angelfishes have spread, evolved and adapted during their approximately 50 million year history.

You will meet different angelfishes in different areas, the Pacific Ocean, the Indian Ocean, or the Atlantic Ocean. The remotely located species have an exotic charm, even though it does not mean they are rare. The grass seems greener, as we say. For example, divers from the U.S.A. may want to see *Centropyge interrupta* and *Chaetodontoplus septentrionalis*, rarely observed species that live in a small range, common only in Japan. They may be less impressed by *Pomacanthus imperator* and *P. semicirculatus* that have a wider distribution. Aquarists in Florida may not want to keep *Holacanthus ciliaris* in their tanks, as it can be seen in the ocean close by. Angelfishes from Southeast Asia and the Indian Ocean are popular among aquarists. You may notice many unfamiliar places and island names when you read this book. Finding the place on a map makes you enjoy reading about your favorite fish. Surely this adds to the sense of exotic charm of angelfishes. The regional differences are not restricted to angelfish of course. You can have an image if you know where certain fishes and invertebrates occur, so that with experience you can guess the location by an underwater photograph without any more information.

Midway Atoll between Japan and Hawaii is a place to meet species from two oceans. Here we see *C. interrupta* and *C. potteri*. P/T. Nakamura (volvox)

Charming fishes live at Cocos Keeling and Christmas Islands near Indonesia. *Centropyge joculator* and the form of *C. flavissimus* on the right occur only there. P/T. Nakamura (volvox)

Such an enormous *Pomacanthus xanthometopon* is likely to be seen only in the Sea. P/T. Nakamura (volvox)

Pomacanthus maculosus swims with composure in the Red Sea.
P/T. Nakamura (volvox)

Observing angelfishes in the ocean is very important for aquarium hobbyists. Normally they are collected in the wild and sent to us, and we should respect these angelfishes. There are several ways to do so. First of all, keep angelfishes with your love, in a suitable habitat with good equipment and proper nutrition until the end of their life. Possibly know their living environment by diving. Meeting with angelfishes under the water you will know their habits, preferred temperature, the brightness of the light, with what kinds of fishes they swim, and the structure of their home territory. This information is instructive for keeping them in an aquarium. Of course, the cost of diving is not cheap. Some aquarists may prefer to invest in the equipment for their aquariums instead of diving. However, one experience of diving will change you. In addition, I suggest that divers have an aquarium too. Maintaining an aquarium helps you to understanding the natural ecosystem. Divers may dislike aquarists because they perceive them as stealing fishes from nature. If divers understood the dedication of aquarists, they could develop a respect for the hobby. Aquarists and divers have a privilege to know the mystery and beauty of the oceans through a love for angelfishes and their habitat.

The size of Angelfishes

Angelfishes include large and small sized species. The size of adults of small-sized genera is less than 10cm. In large-sized genera adults grow 40 to 60cm. These angelfishes are nevertheless not very big compared to other much larger fishes that occur on reefs. The size and swiming style make angelfishes popular in aquariums. They become accustomed to the artificial structures in aquarium aquascapes, and show the same behaviors as in nature.

Classification of Angelfishes

Genus	Subgenus	Characters
Centropyge	Centropyge	Occurring on coral reefs in shallow water. Lips of equal size. Filed teeth on both jaws are for eating polyps of corals.
	Xiphypops	This subgenus adapts to many environments from shallow to deep water. Their varied food preferences make them easy to keep in aquariums. Upper lip hangs over lower lip.
Paracentropyge		The high-bodied Peppermint Angelfish, Multibarred Angelfish, and Purple-mask Angelfish are in the genus *Paracentropyge*.
Genicanthus		This genus swims in mid-water, and is a plankton feeder. The body color differs between males and females, and the males are bigger than females.
Apolemichthys		Mid-sized angelfishes from 20 to 30cm in length, with rounded soft dorsal and anal fins.
Chaetodontoplus		The body shape is a trapezoid or square. The scales are very fine, and the skin is smoother than other angelfishes.
Pygoplites		Only the Regal Angelfish is in this genus. The distinction may be arbitrary, since this species has much in common with members of the genus *Holacanthus*.
Holacanthus	Angelichtys	This subgenus has a unique style, having a dorsal and anal fin with a long filament. The distribution is the Atlantic Ocean. One example is the Queen Angelfish.
	Holacanthus	Only the Rock Beauty is in this subgenus.
	Plitops	This subgenus occurs in a limited area in the East Pacific Ocean, and has the characteristic of living in large groups.
Pomacanthus	Euxiphipops	The Sixbanded Angelfish, Majestic Angelfish, and Blueface Angelfish are this subgenus.
	Pomacanthodes	The Emperor Angelfish, Arabian Angelfish and other famous angelfishes are in this subgenus.
	Pomacanthus	The French Angelfish and Gray Angelfish from the Atlantic Ocean are in this subgenus.

11

Genus *Centropyge*

Members of the Genus *Centropyge* are small and cute, and very popular with aquarists and divers. They swim actively, and are among the fastest moving fishes on the reef. *Centropyge* spp. occur on reefs around the world, with some endemic species found at special areas. So far none have been found on the west coast of Africa nor the west coast of the Americas. The genus is divided into the subgenera *Xiphypops* and *Centropyge*, and the recently erected genus *Paracentropyge* was once included with *Centropyge*, since its members are also small in size.

Centropyge acanthops (Norman 1922)
African Flameback Pygmy Angelfish

The African Flameback Pygmy Angelfish is one of the smallest members of the genus *Centropyge*. The body color is a contrasty combination of orange and dark blue. The largest individuals are almost 8cm, but 4cm is typical. This fish occurs in shallow depths of 10 to 20m. Though small, it is a very tough fish and attacks fishes of the same size. The color does not differ between the sexes. The male is bigger than the female and has a more elongate body, while the female has a more round shape. Five or six individuals make a harem in nature, normally one male, the rest female.

Distribution: East coast of Africa, Mauritius, Seychelles, the Chagos Archipelago and Arabian Peninsula

Centropyge acanthops does not have any regional color morphs. This individual is from Kenya.

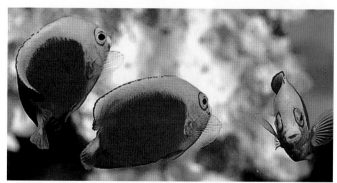

In captivity *C. acanthops* will attack each other. An exception is a pair.

Centropyge aurantonotus Burgess 1974
Caribbean Flameback Pygmy Angelfish

The Caribbean Flameback Pygmy Angelfish strongly resembles the African Flameback Pygmy Angelfish, but the distribution of these fishes is totally different. The African Flameback Pygmy has a colorless caudal fin, while the Caribbean Flameback Pygmy Angelfish has a blue one, the same color as the body. This fish was discovered and reported later than the African Flameback Pygmy Angelfish. The character is similar to the African Flameback Pygmy Angelfish: aggressive despite its small body. Especially the mature ones (males) are very aggressive, and they attain a size slightly larger than *C. acanthops*. This fish is omnivorous, always picking on rocks, and is easy to keep in an aquarium.

Distribution: Brazil and the Southern Caribbean Sea, especially around Barbados and Curacao. It does not occur in Florida nor the Gulf of Mexico.

The difference between this and the former species is mainly the color of the tail. However this difference changes the image of the fish.

Keeping a pair is easy in aquariums.

14

Centropyge argi Wood & Kanazawa 1951
Cherub Angelfish

It is a "Cherub", like a fat pretty child with small wings. The entire body is dark blue, and only the face is orange. Each individual has a different amount of orange area on the face. The behavior and body shapes are similar to the African Flameback Pygmy Angelfish and the Caribbean Flameback Pygmy Angelfish. This fish is one of the most popular fish in aquariums. A strong light makes the body shine metallic blue, while under weak lighting the body looks dull.

Distribution: Caribbean Sea as far south as French Guiana, Western Atlantic to North Carolina, Bermuda, Florida, and the Gulf of Mexico

The orange area differs in each individual. The size is 4.5cm.

This rare individual has a dark blue head.

Centropyge fisheri (Snyder 1904)
Fisher's Pygmy Angelfish

Centropyge fisheri is one of the Cherub type angelfishes that occurs around Hawaii. The body is a dull orange color, with a lighter orange area on the head and anterior portion of the body. A diffuse deep blue spot occurs just behind the gill cover. The Whitetail Pygmy Angelfish (*Centropyge flavicauda*) from Izu Island, Palau and Saipan has the same spot, and these two species are very closely related. In fact they are now considered probable synonyms (Randall, et al., 1997). Fisher's Pygmy Angelfish occurs at depths of 10m to more than 50m in Hawaii. The male has a long body and, the posterior portion of the dorsal fin and anal fin have blue lines.

Distribution: Hawaiian Islands and Johnston Atoll.

The body of males is long. The size is 5cm.

The body of females is round. The size is 3.5cm.

Centropyge flavicauda Fraser-Brunner 1933
Whitetail Pygmy Angelfish

Centropyge flavicauda is dark brown with dark gray on central body sides, but a mature individual turns to a beautiful metallic dark blue. Cherub type angelfishes occur on reefs around the world, and *C. flavicauda* has the widest range in the genus *Centropyge*. Some distinct color morphs are found, and the same color morph appears among different Cherub angelfish types at certain locations. For example *C. flavicauda* in Izu Islands has the large black spot behind the gill cover like *C. fisheri*. These characteristics are not easy to see under water because *C. flavicauda* swims very fast in shady areas. *C. flavicauda* is called "Damsel Angelfishes" based on its appearance and swimming style, which make it resemble the many small damselfishes. The head of *C. flavicauda* in the Maldives is colored orange like *C. acanthops*. The hybrid between these two *Centropyge* may occur in the Indian Ocean. It occurs at depths from 10m to 40m.

Distribution: Central to Western Pacific Ocean, Great Barrier Reef, Tahiti, South East Asia, the Maldives, and East Africa

This male from the Philippines is metallic blue. The size is 4.5cm

An individual from Izu Oshima Island in Japan has a dark spot behind the gill covers. H.Ohunama

This individual from the Maldives has a light orange area on the head.

16

Centropyge resplendens Lubbock & Sankey 1975
Resplendent Pygmy Angelfish

Compared with other Pygmy Angelfish, this species has brighter blue color. It only occurs on Ascension Island in southern Atlantic Ocean. Ascension Island is a British Overseas Territory, but it is not easy to visit for tourists, so many fishes living there including this species are not common in the aquarium trade. Collecting them in the wild has recently become prohibited by law. Even public aquariums have difficulty obtaining these fishes. Because they are very rare in the trade, the price is very expensive now. They were sporadically available recently through the captive breeding efforts of Frank Baensch, who has also created a hybrid cross between this species and *C. fisheri*, and it looks a lot like *C. acanthops*. The Resplendent Pygmy Angelfish lives in a small group in shallow water. The male is bigger than the female and has a longer, more narrow body. The color does not differ between the sexes. Angelfish change sex from female to male as they grow. When keeping several juveniles, the most mature one becomes male within half or one year. The male grows to 6 to 7 cm and becomes aggressive. Unfortunately females are not prevented from becoming males, and the result is that eventually two males occur in a group, and they will fight in an aquarium until one is destroyed. Be careful with tank mates.They quarrel especially over territory against same-sized *Centropyge*, and they tighten their guard against any newcomers. They are omnivores but like to graze on microalgae, and are easy to keep in the aquarium. Under good conditions they spawn daily at dusk. It is ideal to keep a pair of them to see their spawning.

Distribution: Ascension Island

Mature males have an elongate body. The size is 7cm

A small group of *Centropyge resplendens* makes a colony.

Young individuals get along well.

Centropyge loricula (Gunther 1874)
Flame Angelfish

The Flame Angelfish has a red body and black bands with some variation in each individual. Marquesas specimens lack the bands, having a single black spot only. Females have a short, round body. In mature males the soft dorsal fin and anal fin are sharp edged with distinctive blue and black horizontal lines. When a male with these characteristics and much smaller female are kept together in the same aquarium, it is possible to form a pair. You should put the female into the tank first for the female to become acclimated. After 1 or 2 weeks, you can put the male into the tank. This facilitates the formation of a pair and makes less stress to the female because she will be able to defend herself against the newly added but more aggressive male. In nature this fish lives singly or in pairs in reef areas at 15 to 60m depths. Often more than one female is associated with a dominant male. The territory is 1m around a coral outcrop on the reef.

Distribution: Central Pacific to West Pacific, Hawaii, Marquesas, Kiribati, Marshall Is., Great Barrier Reef, and Indonesia

This individual came from Christmas Island. It shows female and the start of male characteristics.

Pair photographed in the Solomon Islands. The female is below right, male upper left. J. Sprung

C. loricula x *C. potteri* hybrid.from Hawaii.

"Ultra flame" from Hawaii.

The black bands are almost invisible in this female from the Marshall Islands.

C. loricula x *C. bispinosa* hybrid.from the Marshall Islands.

C. loricula male with aberrant coloration. It lacks black pigment.

Centropyge shepardi Randall & Yasuda 1979
Shepard's Angelfish, Mango angelfish

Shepard's Angelfish has an orange body with narrow black bands, finer than in *C. loricula*. The number of bands and body color varies. In nature, it occurs in coral reefs and shallow lagoons. Juveniles cannot be found at shallow depths, and usually occur from 20 to 30m. The distribution of *C. shepardi* overlaps with *C. loricula* and *C. bispinosa* and, rarely, they form hybrids.

Distribution: Ogasawara, Guam, Saipan, and Mariana Islands

The vivid reddish orange is a characteristic of *C. shepardi.*

A hybrid from the Philippines looks like a male *C. shepardi*, but is *C. loricula* x *C. ferrugata.*

Juvenile *C. shepardi* with few bands.

Centropyge ferrugata Randall & Burgess 1972
Rusty angelfish

Centropyge ferrugata looks similar to *C. loricula* or *C. shepardi*, but can be distinguished by its fine spots instead of bands, and a gray or brown color extending from the head to dorsal area. Among aquarium hobbyists it is very popular, and most specimens originate from the Philippines and Indonesia. The pattern of spots and body color morphs varies only slightly.

Distribution: South Japan north to Hachizyo Is., Western Pacific, Philippines and Indonesia.

A pattern of spots appears on the body side of *C. ferrugata.*

This individual lacks the black spots and has a white body.

This individual from Indonesia is a hybrid, possibly with *C. bispinosa.*

19

Centropyge bispinosa (Gunther 1860)
Coral Beauty

Among angelfishes, this species has the widest distribution, and it has many kinds of color variants. In the typical form, the head, dorsal, caudal fin, and anal fin are purple, the ventral portion of the body is orange, and irregular fine orange lines occur in the central part of the body sides. Completely orange color morphs occur rarely, but more frequently a solid dark blue color morph occurs. The color variation is not just based on differences among individuals, it is also based on where individuals come from. Dark orange individuals come from the South Pacific, Samoa, and Fiji. Individuals from Mauritius and East India have very fine lines on the caudal fins. However some of the color variants revert to the typical color form in the aquarium over time.

Distribution: Central to East Pacific, South Pacific, Southeast Asia, Great Barrier Reef, Sri Lanka, Maldives, Madagascar, Mauritius, and East Africa

This individual from Indonesia has a beautiful body with a combination of blue and orange.

This rare color morph came from Samoa. The size is 9cm.

This individual came from Mauritius.

This individual came from Indonesia.

Probable *C. bispinosa* x *C. shepardi* hybrid.

This solid blue individual came from Indonesia.

This individual came from the Philippines.

This individual came from Samoa.

The individual came from the Marshall Islands.

Centropyge muliticolor Randall & Wass 1974
Multicolor Pygmy Angelfish

Centropyge muliticolor lives in caves at a 20 m depth mostly. Since this is a difficult habitat for collection it is not easy to find *C. muliticolor* in the aquarium trade, compared with other *Centropyge* spp. Because the Multicolor Pygmy Angelfish occurs in shaded portions of the reef, the dorsal part is white, unlike any other species in the genus. When an individual lives outside of its normal cave habitat, and under strong light in the aquarium, the color of the body becomes darker over time. If you want to keep the white dorsal color, you should keep *C. muliticolor* under fluorescent lighting and include caves in the aquascape. The blue crown on the head and yellowish mouth are not vivid but are an elegant combination. Also the pattern in the crown on the head varies in each individual. The crown of juveniles is small, and it becomes larger as the fish matures. The crown of mature males is bigger and more remarkable than in females. The Multicolor Pygmy Angelfish is omnivorous, so it is easy to feed any food.

Distribution: Marshal Islands, Palau, Fiji, and Cook Islands

Mature male from the Marshall Islands. The size is 7cm.

The same individual as above. The body color is changed by captive conditions.

A female has a round body.

The crown mark is small on juveniles. The size is 3cm.

Centropyge joculator Smith-Vanizl & Randall 1974
Cocos Island Pygmy Angelfish, Joculator Angel

This highly prized angelfish occurs only at Australian
territorial Christmas Island and Cocos-Keeling Island near
Indonesia. Its blue "eyeshadow" is remarkable!
Christmas and Cocos-Keeling are small islands surrounded
by deep ocean. Therefore the environment around the
islands is isolated. For example, in the Indian Ocean,
Centropyge flavissima lives only at these islands. The
scientific name joculater means "a clown" in Latin, and
Centropyge joculator's personality is very lively. *Centropyge
joculator* accepts most foods, so it is easy to keep in an
aquarium. Males have sharp soft dorsal and anal fins with
blue edges.

Distribution: Christmas Island, and Cocos-Keeling Island

Adults grow to 10cm in aquariums.

The color is almost not changed from juveniles to adults. The size is 4cm.

This adult male shows pointed soft dorsal and anal fins, and tail filaments.

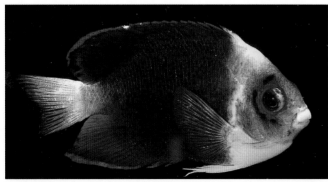
This individual is a rare color morph. The size is 9cm.

Small juveniles have an ocellus on the soft dorsal fin and a slight band marks the eyes. The size is 2.5cm.

Centropyge hotumatua Randall & Caldwell 1973
Hotumatua's Pygmy Angelfish

Centropyge hotumatua lives around the Easter Islands that are famous for the Moai statues. The blue rings around the eyes make it look like the Cocos Pygmy Angelfish, but *C. hotumatua* has an orange face. It is easy to distinguish between these similar species.

Also this species has an eyespot behind the gill and another on the soft dorsal fin. The deep blue area on half of the body varies in each individual, and the color becomes darker in the aquarium over time. The reef is developed well around Easter Islands, despite the fact that the temperature of the sea is not very warm there. A temperature between 22 and 23 degrees Celsius is best for *C. hotumatua*, since 25 degrees Celsius is the upper limit for its original environment. Collectors based in Hawaii collect *C. hotumatua* for the aquarium trade. With a long trip from the Easter Islands, most individuals are stressed on arrival. Basically *C. hotumatua* is active like *C. joculator*. It takes more time to be acclimated to an aquarium, however, and can only be recommended to aquarists with some expert level of technique. When the species is not in good condition, the color is pale, not vivid. The specific name "hotumatua" comes from the famous leader in Polynesia who was the first king to emigrate to the Easter Islands.

Distribution: Austral Islands, Pitcairn, and Easter Island

A well-acclimated and healthy individual has dark color.

The area of dark brown differs in each individual. The size is 4cm.

The color of juveniles is the same as adults. The size is 3cm.

Centropyge abei Allen, Young, & Colin 2006
Deep Water Pygmy Angelfish

This newly discovered species was first observed in Palau at 110-155 m depth using a research submersible, and then in Sulawesi Indonesia at 120 m. The color pattern is reminiscent of the Racon Butterflyfish (*Chaetodon lunula*). The specimens collected seem to have unique physical characteristics not shared by any other angelfish species. So far this fish has been described as a modified *Centropyge* sp., but it may be moved to another genus after further analysis of its features and DNA.

In 2007, a 3cm long juvenile was found and photographed at Miyazaki, Japan at a depth of only 5 meters! Presumably it originated from a spawning in deep water in the Philippines to the south. After continuous observation by divers for 2 months in the 17 °C water, it disappeared.

Distribution: Palau, Indonesia, Japan, and probably widespread in the Western Pacific

This 3cm individual was found at Miyazaki, Japan at a depth of only 5 meters!

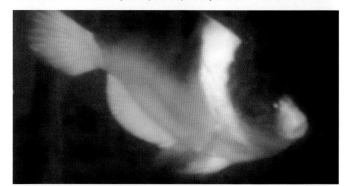
This individual is on display at the Waikiki Aquarium. J.C. Delbeek

Centropyge nahackyi Kosaki 1974
Nahacky's Angelfish

Named after the famous fish collector Tony Nahacky, this rare species has a similar crown to that found in *Centropyge muliticolor*, but in *C. nahackyi* the crown is larger. Nahacky's Angelfish lives only Johnston Atoll, located south of Hawaii, but strays can sometimes be found, very rarely, in the Hawaiian Islands. Whenever a species lives only on the frontier, where there is no tourism, it is very difficult for aquarists to obtain. We hope that in the near future this species will be bred for the aquarium hobby.

Distribution: Johnston Atoll

Juveniles look much like adults.

The marks on the head have different size in each individual. The size is 7cm. M.Kobayashi

This male has a big mark on the head. The size is 6cm. John E. Randall

Centropyge potteri Jordan & Metz 1912
Potter's Angelfish

Centropyge potteri is the most popular Hawaiian Angelfish. Most of the Angelfish that occur in the Hawaiian Islands, *C. potteri, C. fisheri, Apolemichthys arcuatus,* and *Genicanthus personatus* are endemic to the region. It is interesting that also Midway Island is similar to the ecosystem of Hawaii. Potter's Angelfish occurs at depths from a few meters to more than 50 m. From the head to dorsal the body has orange scribbled patterns. Potter's Angelfish has color variants based on the level of maturity. A dark blue area on the ventral part becomes wider with age and size. The area behind gills is dark blue on the mature males. Compared with females, males have a more reddish head. Because the sex can be distinguished by the color morph, it is easy to make a pair in an aquarium. A blue color morph has been found at a depth in excess of 50 m.

Distribution: Hawaiian Islands and Midway Islands

The size is 8cm. The body of a large male has strong contrast of colors.

The body size and color are different between males and females.

This individual is a rare color morph, "Blue Potters."

A first-of-its-kind presumed hybrid cross of *C. potteri* and *C. fisheri* from Hawaii. J. C. Delbeek.

A hybrid with *C. loricula* from Hawaii.

The size of this juvenile is 2cm.

Centropyge interrupta Tanaka 1918
Japanese Pygmy Angelfish, Japanese Angelfish

The Japanese Pygmy Angelfish is the largest member of the genus *Centropyge*, achieving a size of up to 15cm. It is one of the few members of the genus *Centropyge* that occurs on the coast of Japan. *Centropyge interrupta* lives in the Temperate Zone, so it is accustomed to temperatures below 20 °C, and does not fare well above 25 °C. The color of the body changes dramatically with size. Fine blue spots are on the head and dorsal part on Juveniles and young adult females. The blue spots become larger, and connect to each other during the sex change to males. Mature males are deep blue across the head and gills and are more remarkable than females. The male also has more sharply pointed soft dorsal and anal fins, with bright blue horizontal lines on a dark blue background. In nature a pair or a harem occurs, often on rocky reefs, at depths from 15m to 20m. Juveniles smaller than 5 cm, are found in deep water on steep outer reefs. There are 2 key points to keeping *C. interrupta* in an aquarium. One is keeping the temperature under 25 °C. The other is to have a chance to get juveniles. Large individuals are so stressed by capture that they seldom accept foods. This species has been bred and raised in captivity by Frank Baensch.

Distribution: Izu Islands, Coastal South Japan, Ogasawara Islands, and Midway Islands

The distribution of this species is not only in Japan, but also Midway atoll.

The color differs a little in males and females.

This juvenile is 3cm long. The body is a beautiful shining metallic blue.

The size of this juvenile is 1cm.

Centropyge debelius Pyle 1990
Debelius' Angelfish, Blue Mauritius Angelfish

Centropyge debelius was discovered, and recorded only recently. The specific name is to honor the German underwater photographer, author, and aquarist Helmut Debelius. The body color is deep blue, and the head has many deep blue spots against a lighter background. The tail is yellow. In deep water, a young individual with its yellow mouth, pectoral and caudal fins is clear to see. The color pattern looks similar to *C. interrupta and C. nahackyi*. Females have fewer spots, and the blue is not vivid. Males have a lot of spots, and the face is especially blue. Juveniles are an impressive deep blue. There are two reasons it was not discovered until recently. Debelius' Angelfish lives in deep caves on drop-offs, and it does not have bright color. In the aquarium trade, *C. debelius* is very seldom seen.

Distribution: Mauritius and Reunion Islands

This male has a beautiful body. The size is 9cm.

This female has a round body. The size is 7cm.

The size of this young individual is 9cm.

The size of this juvenile with an eyespot is 2.5cm.

Centropyge flavissima (Cuvier 1831)
Lemonpeel Angelfish

Literally *Centropyge flavissima* has bright yellow color like a lemon peel. It is one of the most beautiful *Centropyge* with its blue eye shadow surrounding its yellow eyes. The Lemonpeel Angelfish occurs in coral-rich areas, mainly around oceanic islands. It nips coral polyps and tissues and algae. Many hybrids of *C. flavissima* with other *Centropyge* spp. are reported. Most of the hybrids are with *C. vrolikii* and *C. eibli*. One reason for the various color morphs is this hybridization. At Christmas Island in the Indian Ocean, however, *C. flavissima* has a different color morph compared with *C. flavissima* in the Pacific Ocean. The eye is blue, like in *C. vrolikii*, and it lacks or has a much-reduced blue eye shadow ring. In both forms the juveniles have a big blue-ringed eyespot on the middle of the body. This is a special character for the species.*

Distribution: Middle, West, and South Pacific oceanic islands, Cocos-keeling and Christmas Island in the Indian Ocean, and the Great Barrier Reef

*Note: The juvenile of *Holacanthus tricolor* has essentially the same appearance, a form of convergence.

This typical individual came from the Marshall Islands.

These came from the Marshall Islands. They may have an ancestor that is a hybrid.

This individual came from Christmas Island. The face is not the same as typical individuals from the Pacific Ocean.

The size of this juvenile with an eyespot is 3cm.

28

Centropyge eibli (Klausewitz 1963)
Eibl's Angelfish, Blacktail Angelfish

With orange eye shadow highlighting blue eyes Eibl's
Angelfish is an impressive character. It also sports thin wavy
vertical orange bands on a greenish gray body, an orange
"chest" and a blue-edged black tail. *Centropyge vrolikii* is its
closest relative, and hybrids between them are common. In
many regions the number of hybrids is almost the same as
pure *C. eibli*. The hybrids have a continuous range of color
morphs between the species characters. Some examples have
no bands, or a broader black area. At Christmas Island and
Cocos-Keeling Islands in the Indian Ocean, the especially
beautiful and rare hybrid with *C. flavissima* occurs. The
maximum size is 15 cm (6 in.). The diet consists mainly of
algae, which should be offered in the aquarium, but this
species is omnivorous.

Distribution: Indonesia, North West Australia, Christmas
Island, Sri Lanka, Andaman Sea, and Thailand

This typical individual came from Indonesia.

This hybrid came from Indonesia.

This hybrid individual from Christmas Island looks like *C. flavissima*.

This juvenile from Christmas Island is 3.5cm long.

The color of juveniles is the same as adults.

Centropyge vrolikii (Bleeker 1853)
Halfblack Angelfish, Pearlscale Angelfish

Centropyge vrolikii looks a lot like its close relative *C. eibli*, but lacks the wavy vertical orange bands and has about the rear 1/3 of the body black. This species occurs across a very broad range, from the Western Pacific Ocean to the Great Barrier Reef. Hybrids with *C. eibli* are very common wherever the two species occur. In the Philippines only *C. vrolikii* occurs and consequently there are no hybrids between tem there. The body color of *C. vrolikii* is not vivid, but the white scales and orange eye shadow give this species special character. In the Marshal Islands, many hybrids occur with *C. flavissima*. Examples include *C. flavissima* with a black tail and *C. vrolikii* with light yellowish color. The color variants of hybrids charm us. Maximum size is 12 cm (4.7 in.). The diet consists mainly of algae, which should be offered in the aquarium, but this species is omnivorous.

Distribution: North to Izu Islands in Western Pacific Ocean, South East Asia, Micronesia, Great Barrier Reef, and East Australia

This typical individual came from the Philippines.

This yellowish hybrid individual came from the Marshall Islands.

This aberrant individual from the Great Barrier Reef lacks the black body color.

An unusual hybrid may be *C. vroliki* with *C. bicolor*.

The juvenile has a remarkable large black spot on the gill cover. The size is 2.5cm.

Centropyge **spp.** and Mimic tangs

There are Tangs that occur in the same distribution with *Centropyge* spp. in which the juveniles have body coloration and shape extremely like their *Centropyge* spp models. They are called "Mimic Tangs." Juveniles of *Acanthurus tristis* imitate *C. eibli* exactly. Adults of this species are dark brown. Why does this occur? there must be some benefit for this mimicry to have evolved. Can the Mimic Tang achieve protection from its enemies by mimicry? I do not think so. *Centropyge* spp. are aggressive toward others of their kind to keep their own territory, so Mimic Tangs are attacked by their *Centropyge* spp. models. Juveniles of *Acanthurus pyroferus* are another example with even greater talent. This species has 3 color morphs. Juveniles can look like *C. flavissima, C. herraldi,* or *C. vrolikii.* Still we do not know what is the benefit of this mimicry!

Indian Ocean Mimic Tang known as "Eibli Tang," shown with its model below.

Acanthurus pyroferus (yellow type), right, and *Centropyge heraldi*, left.

Adult of *Acanthurus pyroferus.*

Centropyge heraldi Woods & Schultz 1953
Herald's Angelfish, False Lemonpeel

Centropyge heraldi looks like *C. flavissima* because both
species have a vivid yellow body color. Within the yellow in
C. heraldi there is a subtle pattern of light orange and green.
Not all *C. heraldi* are yellow, however. Many distinct color
morphs are found. In Fiji and Tonga, the color morph has a
black saddle on the back of the dorsal fin. The black saddle
varies in size, sometimes reaching the central part of the
dorsal fin, sometimes very small. In the Philippines,
sometimes there are individuals with brown faces and black
or dark tail, and dorsal area. One hypothesis suggests that
these individuals are hybrids with *C tibicen*. However, when
some of these individuals are kept in the aquarium, they
become a normal color morph with time. For this reason, I
believe it is not a hybrid but simply one of the range of color
morphs in this variable species.

Distribution: North to Hachijo Islands in the Western Pacific
Ocean, Micronesia, Coral Sea, Fiji, and Tonga

This individual came from the Philippines. The size is 6cm.

This individual came from Fiji. The size is 5cm.

This individual came from Tonga. The size is 7cm.

This individual came from the Philippines.
The size is 7cm.

This individual came from the Philippines.
The size is 5cm.

Centropyge tibicen (Cuvier 1831)
Keyhole Angelfish

The Keyhole Angelfish gets its common name from the remarkable white spot in the center of its nearly all-black body. The edges of its pelvic fins and anal fin are yellow, and a dark bluish spot occurs between the gill and white spot. The white spot is very visible underwater, and is not the same on each individual. The white spot becomes smaller as the fish grows. Mature males are deep blue, and impressive. In Japan *Centropyge tibicen* often occurs on rocky reefs in Hachijo and Wakayama. The Keyhole Angelfish seems to be one of the more popular species in aquariums, and is hardy when given an adequate supply of algae to graze. The maximum size is 19 cm (about 7.5 inches), making it the largest member of the genus, with *C. interruptus* a close second.

Distribution: North to Chiba in Western Pacific Ocean, Izu Islands, Philippines, Indonesia, and Australia

The white spot in adults is smaller than juveniles. The size is 8cm.

The size is 5cm.

Aberrant adult individual. J. Chua.

Centropyge nox (Bleeker 1853)
Midnight Angelfish

Centropyge nox is an unusual dark black species with a tall body. It is not easy to believe at first, but this black body is good camouflage on the reef. The sun's rays make many shadows in cracks and crevices in the reef. It swims in these shadows, so divers cannot see the black body. Juveniles have a yellow small spot on the pectoral fins. Rare specimens are solid yellow, or have a "koi" pattern of yellow, black, gray, and white. It occurs on rich coral reefs and picks on polyps or the surface of corals. The Midnight Angelfish sometimes refuses to feed, but fares well in aquariums with live rock upon which it can graze on algae. The maximum size is 10 cm (about 4 inches).

Distribution: North to Okinawa, the Philippines, Indonesia, and Great Barrier Reef

The whole body is totally black. The size is 6cm.

Large adult with aberrant coloration. J. Sprung

Juveniles have a spot above the pectoral fins.

Centropyge bicolor (Bloch 1787)
Bicolor Angelfish

Centropyge bicolor has beautiful contrasting coloration, with bright yellow and dark blue that looks black in dull light. Tiny juveniles have lighter vertical bands within the blue area. Compared with other *Centropyge* spp., *C. bicolor* has an unusual body shape. The dorsal and anal fins are sharply pointed and develop filaments. This trait is seen in other angelfish genera, especially in *Holacanthus*. The Bicolor Angelfish occurs among small coral heads and on rubble slopes in rich coral reef areas, and is exceedingly abundant in the Western Pacific Ocean. Among *Centropyge* spp, *C. bicolor* has the biggest cheek spines. Mature individuals have a platinum band on the boundary between the yellow and blue parts. Attaining a maximum size of about 15cm, *C. bicolor* is one of the larger *Centropyge* spp. The Bicolor Angelfish is not aggressive and tends to be delicate in the aquarium. Keeping it with large aggressive or predatory fishes is not a good idea. Hybrids and special color morphs of this species are very rare. Only some reports of regional color morphs were shown from the Great Barrier Reef.

Distribution: North to Wakayama in the Western Pacific Ocean; Philippines, Indonesia, Malaysia, North Western Australia, Great Barrier Reef, New Caledonia, Samoa

This individual came from the Philippines. The size is 10cm.

This individual that has a yellow dorsal fin came from Indonesia.

A rare color morph individual from the Great Barrier Reef.

The size of this juvenile is 3cm.

Centropyge flavipectoralis Randall & Klausewitz 1977
Yellowfin Angelfish

Centropyge flavipectoralis has a cute yellow pectoral fin that contrast its dark nearly black body color. Dark black fish hide easily in the coral reef. Therefore this fish is not commonly observed or collected. Once you observe it for a while, you may feel this species' subtle colors. However the whole body of matured males develops an amazing metallic blue sheen, which requires strong lighting to fully appreciate in an aquarium. *Centropyge flavipectoralis* has a specific body shape with a longer dorsal fin and anal fin, much like *C. bicolor*. Juveniles have black bands, and resemble *Centropyge multispinis*. Maximum size 10 cm.

Distribution: Central Indian Ocean including Sri Lanka and the Maldives

The body of this male is metallic blue. The size is 7cm.

Centropyge multispinis Playfair & Gunther 1867
Manyspined Angelfish

Centropyge multispinis has faintly visible thin bands on the body and a black spot next to the gill.Å@Unfortunately these color patterns are not so remarkable because of the dark body which dulls them. Only the metallic blue on the pelvic fin is a good point to distinguish this species from other black *Centropyge* spp. A golden color morph of this species occurs sometimes. However in an aquarium, this morph becomes the normal color. It is not known why this golden color morph occurs in this species. Maximum size 9 cm.

Distribution: Central Indian Ocean including Sri Lanka and the Maldives, east to western Thailand, Western Indian Ocean, East Afriica and the Red Sea

The blue ventral fin is remarkable. The size is 6cm.

Xanthic form. The size is 9cm.

Xanthic form. The size is 8cm. N. Hashimoto

Centropyge colini Smith-Vaniz & Randall 1974
Colin's Angelfish

Centropyge colini likes to live in caves and among complicated reef structures at depths in excess of 20m. Sometimes swimming upside-down in caves, *C. colini* prefers dark places, so it does not occur on a bright coral reef. The body color is light metallic blue dorsally and transparent yellow or green ventrally. Compared with other *Centropyge* spp., it has a higher body. The dorsal fin is longer and with sharp spines. The personality is gentle, and sensitive. It is a shy fish that takes time to venture out in the open in an aquarium. It should be kept with less aggressive feeders since it does not compete well for food, and it needs cooler temperature, not more than 25 °C. Maximum size is 9cm.

Distribution: Philippines, Indonesia, Cocos- Keeling Island, Palau, Guam, Marshal Islands, and Fiji.

This individual came from Indonesia. The size is 5cm.

This juvenile came from the Philippines. The size is 2cm.

Centropyge narcosis Pyle & Randall 1992
Narc Angelfish

Centropyge narcosis has a an amazing yellow body color. This rare species occurs at depths in excess of 100m. The body shape and personality is similar to *C. colini*. It also lives in caves on steep drop-offs. Right now *C. narcosis* is known only from the Cook Islands. There is a high probability it lives other places. If one can have a chance to get *C. narcosis*, it should be kept in a dimly illuminated aquarium under blue light. Too bright a light source makes this species stressed and it dulls the body color. The temperature should be maintained cooler, about 22-24 °C maximum.

Distribution: Cook Islands

The black spot on the body appears in juveniles and adults. The size is 4.5cm.

The spiny rays of the dorsal fin are distinctive.

Centropyge aurantia Randall & Wass 1974
Golden Angelfish

Centropyge aurantia is called "Golden", but the body color looks like copper more than gold. There is some variation as specimens can be more brownish or more orange. *Centropyge aurantia* is difficult to see in the ocean. It occurs on rich coral reefs, but is most likely to be spotted only among piles of dead coral. This species eats coral polyps and tissues, as well as algae. The personality is shy and it doesn't venture out in open spaces. The Golden Angelfish is very unique in *Centropyge* spp. The body shape is rounded, the mouth is tiny, and the face is so cute. Maximum size is 10cm.

Distribution: Western Pacific, Solomon Islands, Samoa, East Indonesia and Great Barrier Reef

Typical individual at 4.5cm.

Darker individual. The size is 5cm.

Brightly colored individual. The size is 4cm.

Centropyge nigriocella Woods & Schultz 1953
Blackspot Pygmy Angelfish

Centropyge nigriocella is poorly known despite being widely distributed. It has a very cautious disposition and hides deeply in coral rubble whenever it sees divers. Not many pictures have been taken of it, and very few have ever been collected. Those that have been collected were obtained with chemicals used to drive it from the dense coral rubble. The body color is plain light greenish yellow with two black spots. One black spot is on pectoral fin base, and the other is toward the lower part of the soft dorsal fin. Maximum size is 6cm.

Distribution: Central to Western Pacific Ocean, Mariana Islands, Admiralty Is., Samoa, Society Is., Line Is., and Johnston Is.

Centropyge nigriocella is rarely photographed. Richard Pyle

Genus *Paracentropyge*

This genus contains 3 species, and it is a new group separated from *Centropyge* after *Paracentropyge boylei* was discovered. The genus *Paracentropyge* has a higher body than *Centropyge,* and its body shape is more square in outline. It occurs along drop-offs in or adjacent to deep water, and it is difficult to find. New species in this group will surely be discovered in the near future.

Paracentropyge boylei (Pyle & Randall 1992)
Peppermint Angelfish

Once you've seen it, the beautiful *Paracentropyge boylei* will never be lost from your memory. It was discovered only recently because it lives at 130m depths, where regular scuba diving is not an option. The deep-water species like *Paracentropyge boylei* are collected, but only rarely, by expert divers with new technology, for example mixed gas and closed-circuit re-breather scuba. In addition, to obtain fish in good condition for an aquarium, special collecting and decompression skills are required. The collected fishes are decompressed in small, pressurized containers placed in shallow water. They would die due to an expansion of their air bladder without an appropriate decompression period. Peppermint Angelfish have among the highest value as aquarium fishes due to the difficulty involved in obtaining them and their extreme beauty. *Paracentropyge boylei* is sensitive and delicate in an aquarium. Nevertheless, when properly collected and cared for, long term success is reported for this species. The temperature must be maintained between 22 and 23 °C. Also the water quality should be maintained to the same standards as for keeping corals in an aquarium. Males have a black edge on a longer dorsal fin and anal fin, and longer ventral fins. Females have a rounder shaped body without a black edge. From these characteristics it is easy to distinguish sex and form pairs in this species. Maximum size is 7 cm.

Distribution: Rarotonga, Cook Islands

The combination of red and white is beautiful. The size is 5cm.

The scientific name honors Chip Boyle who discovered this species.

It is not difficult to keep a pair of *P. boylei* in a tank if you have a male and female.

Paracentropyge multifasciata (Smith & Radcliffe 1911)
Multi-Barred Angelfish

Paracentropyge multifasciata is a beautiful *Paracentropyge* species that is aptly named with its multiple bands. It does not occur on horizontal coral reef areas, but is common in caves or sometimes out in the open along cliff-like edges that separate the reef from a deep drop off, or along steep slopes usually below 20m depth, but often much shallower. Compared to other members in the genus, its habitat is not very deep. Though males are larger than females, distinguishing the sex by appearance is not easy. However there are regional color morphs. Indonesia and Philippine specimens have more bands, and the white area is narrow between the bands. Fiji and Great Barrier Reef morphs have fewer bands, and the black diffuse "eye" spot (ocellus) on the edge of the soft dorsal fin remains even in mature specimens. Juveniles have blue in the eye spot. The Western Pacific variant has 6 or 7 bands in juveniles. The number of bands increases with size. Some adults have more than 10 bands. Maximum size is 12 cm.

Distribution: Central to Western Pacific Ocean, Cocos-Keeling Island, Great Barrier Reef, Fiji, Solomon Islands, and Society Islands

This individual came from the Philippines. The size is 8cm.

This individual with a different coloration came from Fiji. The size is 5cm.

This hybrid with *P. venusta* came from the Philippines. T. Ieda

This individual came from the Philippines. The size is 3cm.

Paracentropyge venusta (Yasuda & Tominaga 1969)
Purplemask Angelfish

Paracentropyge venusta has a beautiful contrasting coloration of yellow and dark blue. Originally classified as a member of the Genus *Holacanthus*, its taxonomic status was later changed to *Centropyge*, which is the present valid name, "Centropyge venustus." I chose to use the name *Paracentropyge venusta*, based on the revision that created the new genus, and recent DNA evidence (Bellwood, et al., 2004). Like other members in the genus, the Purplemask Angelfish occurs in caves along steep reef slopes and reef drop offs. The color and pattern varies in individuals. The dark blue part is on the head (the mask), and the dorsal area to the caudal fin. These dark blue parts are separated on some individuals, while others have one large dark blue area on the dorsal part. It is not known whether the difference is related to the sex. Mature ones usually have a large navy area, so it may be a male characteristic. *Paracentropyge venusta* is one of the more delicate angelfish, and although apparently healthy, most aquarium specimens are so traumatized by capture that they don't feed. Sometimes *Paracentropyge venusta* is handled well and arrives in such superb condition that it eats foods quickly. It likes to feed on live worms, but will adapt to dry foods. It picks on fleshy corals (ie *Trachyphyllia, Cynarina*). *Paracentropyge venusta* prefers dark places and should be provided with an aquascape that includes ledges or caves. It nevertheless easily becomes accustomed to life in reef tanks with metal halide lighting systems. The color does not become dull/dark, and *P. venusta* shows its beautiful color best. The hybrid between *P. venusta* and *P. multifasciata* occurs. Maximum size is 12 cm.

Distribution: Izu Islands, Ryukyu Islands, and Philippines

This color morph is rare. The size is 6cm.

A juvenile has the same body color as adults. The size is 2.5cm.

This individual has a large purple area.

This individual has a small purple area.

Genus *Genicanthus*

Members of the genus *Genicanthus* are called "Swallowtail Angelfishes" due to their exceptional tails that have elongate appendages. Their special features compared to other angelfishes include a streamlined body that gives them high speed swimming ability, and strong differences in appearance between the sexes. During sex change from female to males, the body shape and color changes dramatically. Their behavior is also unique. All species in *Genicanthus* form harem groups, and occur in open water above reefs where they feed on plankton, usually at deep depths. For success with an aquarium specimen, it has to be caught without any stress, and the decompression must be done well. The key point to keeping *Genicanthus* in aquariums is the collecting conditions. The decompression damage suffered by small juvenile fish is less than that in the large adult males. Because of the stress and damage, adult males often fail to adapt to aquariums, refusing to eat, or suffering from buoyancy problems and disease. It is best to try a group of females, and wait for the sex change to occur in the aquarium. Keeping a pair of *Genicanthus* looks wonderful in an aquarium. Some species of *Genicanthus* are attractive to aquarists because one can observe the transition of 3 types of color pattern as they grow from juvenile to young female to adult male. Sex reversal back to female from male is reported in aquariums in *Genicanthus*, but is not known in other angelfish genera, nor from observations in the wild.

Genicanthus spinus Randall 1975
Pitcairn Angelfish

This unusual *Genicanthus* sp. occurs only in a limited area in the South Pacific Ocean. *Genicanthus spinus* swims at 30m depth, so photos are not often taken. The body color on females is a simple metallic light blue. Males have black bands on the dorsal area and the caudal fin has irregular black spots. When comparing only males, *G. spinus* looks like *Genicanthus semicinctus* from Lord Howe Island. Because it is a swimming type fish that does not "hole up" easily in the reef, collecting *G. spinus* by hand net is difficult. Maximum size is 35 cm. Because it occurs in a temperate reef region, cooler water temperature should be maintained in the aquarium: not more than 24 °C.

Distribution: Rarotonga in Cook Islands, the Pitcairn Islands, and Austral Islands

This male came from the Cook Islands. The size is 25cm.

The female has a simple body color. The size is 22cm.

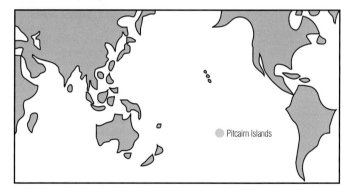

Pitcairn Islands

Genicanthus caudovittatus (Gunther 1860)
Zebra Angelfish

Males of *Genicanthus caudovittatus* have many bands on the whole body. This beautiful angelfish is one of the representative Angelfish found in the Red Sea. The color pattern in males is similar to *G. melanospilos* in the Pacific Ocean. The male Zebra Angelfish has more sharply defined bands and s yellow-bordered dark area on the dorsal fin. Females of *Genicanthus caudovittatus* are completely different from *G. melanospilos*. They are very interesting to aquarists. Juveniles smaller than 4 cm are a pale white with a black eye band, and look quite a bit like *G. personatus*. Maximum size is 20 cm.

Distribution: Red Sea, East Africa, Mauritius, Maldives, and Sri Lanka

The male swims with *Pseudanthias squamipinnis* at a strong current point in Red Sea.

The male characteristic coloration starts to appear on a female.

The female has a bluish white body color. The size is 7cm.

The size of this juvenile is 3cm.

Genicanthus melanospilos (Bleeker 1857)
Blackspot Angelfish

Genicanthus melanospilos and *G. caudovittatus* have a similar color and pattern, but their distributions are separated by Indonesia. *Genicanthus melanospilos* is called Blackspot Angelfish based on one big spot on the abdomen in males. "Yaito Yakko" is Japanese name for *G.Å@melanospilos* based on the male's color. "Yaito" means branded by a hot iron. *Genicanthus melanospilos* is a popular aquarium species, along with the other common *Genicanthus* species from the same region, *G. lamarck*. Hybrids between *Genicanthus melanospilos* and *G. Lamarck* occur, but are rare.

Distribution: Western Pacific Ocean, the Philippines, Indonesia, Papua New Guinea, and the Great Barrier Reef.

This mature male has long tail filaments. T.Nakamura (volovox)

The female and juvenile do not have patterns on the yellow dorsal area.

This individual has strange patterns, and may be a hybrid with *G. lamarck* or *G. semifasciatus*.

This individual also appears to be a hybrid.

Genicanthus lamarck (Lacepeda 1802)
Lamarck's Angelfish

In Japan, *G. lamarck* is called "Tatejima Yakko" from the lateral stripes. "Tatejima" means vertical stripes in Japanese because Japanese name fishes when the fish's head is facing up. Lamarck's Angelfish occurs in relatively shallow depths of about 10m, and is commonly observed by scuba divers on reefs. The coloration in males and females is almost the same. Females have one wide band reaching to the caudal fin, and males lose the wide band. Males have a yellowish forehead mark and black ventral fins. *Genicanthus lamarck* is a popular aquarium fish, and it often is collected from the Philippines and Indonesia. Mature males are difficult to find for sale. Juveniles are easy to keep, and are the best choice. The maximum size is 23 cm. The distribution of Lamark's angelfish is similar to that of *Genicanthus melanospilos*.

Distribution: Western Pacific Ocean, Philippine, Indonesia, Papua New Guinea, and the Great Barrier Reef

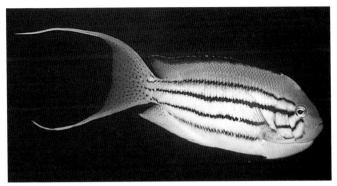

This full sized adult is 28cm long.

This juvenile came from the Philippines. The size is 3cm.

A hybrid with *G. semifasciatus* observed at Izu Ohsima Island in Japan. H. Ohnuma

Genicanthus watanabei Lubbock & Sankey 1975
Watanabe Angelfish

Genicanthus watanabei has a beautiful metallic blue body. Females have black lines on the head, and bright black and white lines appear on the abdomen of the male. During the transition from female to male, the lines on the abdomen show up, and the bands on the head disappear. The balance of hormone in the body affects the color on the body directly. If only one male is in the aquarium, or fails in health, it becomes female. The size does not matter, and hormone balance influenced by the environment is important to determine the sex. Therefore sometimes a small male is found. The Watanabe Angelfish occurs deeper than *G. melanospilos* and *G. lamarck* and it is common for collected specimens to have buoyancy problems. Collectors often use a needle to release gas from the swim bladder as they bring this fish from deep water to the surface. This technique requires skill to do properly. The maximum size is 15cm.

Distribution: Western Pacific Ocean, Philippine, Micronesia, and Great Barrier Reef

This beautiful male came from the Philippines. The size is 14cm.

This female having a darker blue body came from the Philippines. The size is 7cm.

This individual may be a hybrid with *Genicanthus lamarck* at Ogasawara in Japan. O. Morishita

Genicanthus bellus Randall 1975
Ornate Angelfish, Bellus Angelfish

Genicanthus bellus has a unique pattern on the body. Both males and females are beautiful and popular among Aquarium hobbyists. The change color from females to males is veiled in mystery. It must occur quickly, which is surprising considering the big change in pattern and color. G. bellus occurs on reef slopes, deeper than most other *Genicanthus* spp., normally at 40m depth. Like G. *watanabei* the deep origin means this fish often suffers from imperfect decompression. It cannot survive in an aquarium without a perfect decompression. Some of them with buoyancy problems have a swollen abdomen and swim just below the surface, looking toward the bottom most of time. This condition stresses the fish a lot, and it expends a lot of energy fighting to keep from floating to the top. It is important to confirm normal swimming behaviour before buying this and other *Genicanthus* spp. The Ornate Angelfish is expensive because it is collected at deep depth, and requires expert technique and effort to produce a healthy fish for aquariums. Juveniles of G. *bellus* adapt well to aquariums. Wild-harvested adult males do not adapt well and often don't feed. The maximum size is 17cm.

Distribution: Okinawa, Philippines, Indonesia, Cocos Keeling Islands, Marshall Islands, and Tahiti

This male came from the Philippines. The size is 15cm.

An individual during the sex changing period. The size is 8cm.

This female came from Indonesia. The size is 5cm.

Genicanthus semifasciatus (Kamohara 1934)
Japanese Swallow Angelfish

Because the body color is completely different between the sexes in *Genicanthus* spp., males and females of the same species were mistakenly classified first as different species. One example is the Japanese Swallow Angelfish *Genicanthus semifasciatus*. Along with *Centropyge interrupta* and *Chaetodontoplus septentrionalis*, *G. semifasciatus* is one of the famous Japanese angelfishes. The main distribution of *G. semifasciatus* in Japan is the Izu islands, Wakayama, and Shikoku. The Japanese Swallow Angelfish prefers the Temperate Zone in Japan more than the Ryuukyu islands, which are in the Tropical Zone. When the water temperature falls below 20°C during the winter, *G. semifasciatus* moves deeper. The Japanese Swallow Angelfish occurs at 20m depths during the entire year in Hatchizyo Island. Mature males have a yellowish head and a yellowish band reaching the center on the body sides. The beautiful orange bands on the dorsal area look like tiger stripes, and they make this species look more attractive than rarer fishes. For the aquarium trade, it comes from the Philippines. *Genicanthus semifasciatus* from the Temperate Zone mature more slowly than tropical ones. The males of *G. semifasciatus* from the Philippines are smaller than ones from the Temperate Zone. In a similar way, *Pomacanthus imperator* and *Pomacanthus semicirculatus* from the Tropical Zone change their color earlier than ones from the Temperate Zone. The expected reason is that the temperature affects the growth rate. However the temperature in the aquarium should be the same as the temperature of the region where the fish is collected. The maximum size is 21 cm.

Distribution: Western Pacific north to Izu Islands, Taiwan and the Philippines

This male with beautiful irregular tiger patterns came from the Philippines. The size is 12cm.

This individual showing the start of the sex change. The size is 12cm.

This juvenile came from Hachijo Island in Japan. The size is 3.5cm.

52

Genicanthus semicinctus (Waite 1900)
Halfbanded Angelfish

The Halfbanded Angelfish gets its name from the distinctive vertical bands that end midway on the body of the male. The male's body color is beige, yellow on the abdomen, with a stunning blue mouth. Thre is a comical yellow polkadot pattern on the chest, and black spots on the tail. Females have a charcoal gray dorsal area, a white abdomen, and elegant blue eye highlights. Large females develop a blue forehead. *Genicanthus semicinctus* occurs around Lord Howe Island near Queensland in Australia. It does not occur on the rich coral reefs located in the bays of Lord Howe Island, but is found instead on offshore rocky reefs at a depth of 20m. Usually *Genicanthus* spp. form a harem of females with one male. The Halfbanded Angelfish is an exception, Males and females live only individually. In nature, 4 to 5 individuals are found at one place. *Genicanthus semicinctus* is not traded for aquarium hobbyists because Lord Howe Island is a UNESCO World Heritage site. The Australian government protects the animals of Lord Howe Island. The only possibility of the obtaining this species is from outside of the protected area. In any case since adults of any *Genicanthus* sp. are so easily damaged, the best way to see *G. semicinctus* is underwater at Lord Howe Island. It is one of the best diving places, and heaven on earth for angelfish lovers; *Genicanthus semicinctus*, *Chaetodontoplus ballinae*, and *Chaetodontoplus conspicillatus* meet with you there. Maximum size is 30 cm, but the tail filaments may extend the length even further.

Distribution: Lord Howe Island and Kermadec Islands

A male at Balls Pyramid near Lord Howe Island. The size is 27cm. T. Nakamura (volvox)

The female has a unique body color. The size is 18cm. T. Nakamura (volvox)

This female swims with a group of other fishes. T. Nakamura (volvox)

A male at Midway Atoll.
P/T. Nakamura (volvox)

The male, above, has changed sex in
the tank. The size is 14cm.

Genicanthus personatus Randall 1975
Masked Angelfish

Genicanthus personatus is one of the rarest species of *Genicanthus* with impressive white pearl color. It occurs in the Northwestern Hawaiian Islands at depths in excess of 70m, but at Midway Atoll this species is found at a depth of 20m. The temperature of the water at Midway Atoll is lower than Hawaii because of prevailing currents, so the shallow water in Midway Atoll has the same conditions as the deep water in Hawaii. A travel tour to Midway Atoll from Hawaii is one possibility to see *G. personatus*. Midway Atoll is a military territory, so going there is not easy. Therefore *G. personatus* is very expensive if it is ever available for aquariums. Juveniles and young adults (females) have black masks. The black mask of the female fades with size or the beginning of sex change from female to male. The same time, white ventral fins turn to yellow. Finally the masks turn to orange, and an orange line covers the edge of body. Mainly the body color does not change. However the color of mask changes, so the scientific name was given. "Personatus" means "mask" The first *G. personatus* was found in 1972. It was a female. A male was found 3 years later. Recently the number of *G. personatus* has been decreasing in Hawaii. This species' living areas are kept in a National Park. We should see this species at Public aquariums such as the Waikiki Aquarium, and in photographs because a large *Genicanthus* sp. is difficult to deliver to aquariums. Visiting Midway Atoll is another choice for meeting *G. personatus*. A single Masked Angelfish was raised in captivity from a spawning pair at the Waikiki Aquarium. Perhaps this species will become available to the aquarium hobby or public aquariums through captive breeding efforts. Maximum length is 21 cm.

Distribution: Hawaii islands and Midway Atoll

The ventral fin on this individual turned yellow. The size is 14cm.

This female has a white ventral fin. The size is 10cm.

This individual was raised from a spawning pair at the Waikiki Aquarium. The size is 2.5cm.

Genus *Apolemichthys*

The maximum body size of this genus is 25 cm, which makes *Apolemichthys* a midsize group in the angelfishes. They are similar to members of the genus *Holacanthus*, but the body outline is round, and the color in most species is subtle, not vivid. The patterns and subdued coloration gives a unique atmosphere to the fish. *Apolemichthys* spp. occur from shallow coral rich reefs to deep rocky reefs. Most *Apolemichthys* spp. occur at the border of where *Pomacanthus* spp. occur, or deeper, except for the wide ranging species *A. trimaculatus*. *Apolemichthys* spp. have smaller size, and avoid the larger angelfish by occupying a different living area. There is still a chance to find new species of *Apolemichthys* in deep water for this reason.

Apolemichthys trimaculatus (Lacepeda 1831)
Three-spot Angelfish, Flagfin Angelfish

Apolemichthys trimaculatus is the most common species of the genus. It occurs across a wide range, from the Pacific Ocean to the Indian Ocean. Unlike other members of the genus, *A. trimaculatus* has a vivid yellow body color. Yellow angelfishes seem to form hybrids with other species frequently. For example, *Centropyge flavissima* hybridizes with several other *Centropyge* spp. It is not surprising that hybrids between *A. trimaculatus* and other *Apolemichthys* spp. are observed. *Apolemichthys armitagei* was described initially as a new species from the Maldives, and then it was confirmed that it is the hybrid cross between *A. trimaculatus* and *A. xanthurus*. Hybrids of *Apolemichthys trimaculatus* with *A. xanthopunctatus* in Christmas Island, and with *A. kingi* in Africa are also reported These species seem to have a common ancestor. *Apolemichthys trimaculatus, A. griffisi, A. xanthopunctus,* and *A. kingi* have a unique shared mark. Black spots above the eyes look like Japanese court nobles' makeup during the Heian Period. Aquarists in Japan get an image of court nobles' faces from *A. trimaculatus.* The Japanese name for this species comes from the total number of black spots above the eyes and behind the gill, which is actually four in adult specimens, not three. The scientific name, *trimaculatus* means three spots, based on the pattern on the juvenile, which has one spot on the forehead. This one spot separates to two spots as the fish matures. The maximum size is 25 cm.

Distribution: Central to West Pacific, Indonesia, Maldives, Madagascar, and East Africa

This individual came from the Philippines. The size is 14cm.

The juvenile has a black spot on the dorsal fin. The size is 4cm.

The hybrid; "*A. armitagei*" from the Maldives. The size is 12cm.

Juvenile of the hybrid, "*A. armitagei*" from the Maldives. The size is 3cm.

Apolemichthys xanthurus (Bennett 1832)
Yellowtail angelfish, Indian Yellowtail Angelfish

Apolemichthys xanthurus is called "Black Three-spot Angelfish" in Japan. It has a dark beige monochrome aspect composed of a reticulated pattern, contrasted by black soft dorsal and anal fins and a yellow tail. The scientific name refers to the yellow on the caudal fin. Pale yellow "ears" are located at the top of the gills. Small juveniles have a distinct black bar through the eye, which fades a little with size, but the body color does not change much from juvenile to adult. The maximum size of mature adults is small, just 15 cm. *Apolemichthys xanthurus* has a limited distribution. It is common only in the Maldives, but rare in other parts of its range. Despite the lack of color, it is a popular aquarium fish, not aggressive to others. In nature, 5 or 6 individuals often make a colony; keeping 5 or 6 individuals in an aquarium may be a fun. *Apolemichthys xanthurus* is shy and sensitive, so large, more aggressive angelfishes should not be kept with it in a small aquarium.

Distribution: Maldives, Sri Lanka, and East India

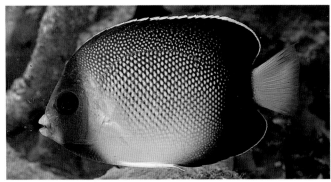
This individual came from the Maldives. The size is 12cm.

This individual came from the Maldives. The size is 6cm.

This individual came from the Maldives. The size is 3cm.

Apolemichthys xanthotis (Fraser-Brunner 1951)
Yellow-ear Angelfish

Apolemichthys xanthotis is also called the "Red Sea Angelfish." It looks like Red Sea variant of *A. xanthurus*, but it has brighter color, with more vivid yellow tail, brighter yellow "ears," and broader more distinct black areas that contrast better with a brighter white body. The Yellow-ear Angelfish occurs in the Red Sea and around the Arabian Peninsula, but does not occur in East Africa. Adults have black spines on the gills. Juveniles have yellow lips and look like *Chaetodontoplus mesoleucus*. The body color is a beautiful bright white even in the adults. However A. xanthotis is not popular in the aquarium trade, and is only rarely collected for aquariums. Maximum size is 15 cm.

Distribution: Red Sea, Persian Gulf, and Gulf of Oman

A. xanthotis swims among reef corals in the Red Sea. T. Nakamura (volvox)

The adult grows up to 15cm.

The mouth of the juvenile is yellow, and the juvenile resembles *Chaetodontoplus mesoleucus.*

Apolemichthys arcuatus (Gray 1831)
Bandit Angelfish, Blackbanded Angelfish

Apolemichthys arcuatus is one of the classic beautiful angelfishes. It was originally described as a *Holacanthus* species, and some ichthyologists have suggested that it should be given status as a new independent genus, *Desmoholacanthus*. The body is not colorful, but it has an elegant and a daring figure, and the contrast of white and black is remarkable viewed underwater or in aquariums. *Apolemichthys arcuatus* normally occurs at depths below 20m in Hawaii, but at only 10m at Midway Atoll. The number of *A. arcuatus* has been decreasing recently, the same as with *Genicanthus personatus*. Commercial aquarium fishermen have set limits on the collection of these rare angelfishes to protect them. A beige area is above the band, and the abdomen is pale white. The body color is not changed much from juveniles to adults, though the black band covers the face and mouth in juveniles. The mouth turns white as the fish grows, and then the white area comes together between the eyes. The small juveniles are popular among aquarium hobbyists, and they occur in rocky areas at great depth. Catching the juveniles is difficult because they do not come out from the shade. Adults are easy to collect because they are slow swimmers. The natural diet includes sponges and algae. The Bandit Angelfish is not easy to feed in aquariums. Smaller specimens adapt better and are more likely to feed. The ideal size of *A. arcuatus* for aquariums is 10cm. The maximum size is 18 cm.

Distribution: Hawaii islands, Johnston Atoll, and Midway Atoll

This adult has an excellent body color. The size is 13cm.

Different sized individuals can be kept in the same tank.

The juvenile's black banding differs from an adult's. T. Ishiwata

Apolemichthys griffisi (Carlson and Taylor 1981)
Griffis Angelfish

One white band on the back is the characteristic mark of
A. griffisi. The body color is gray, and the mouth area is
pale blue or purple in adults. The unique color of
A. griffisi does not change much from juveniles. Juveniles
look like small adults. They have a vertical bar through the
eye, which becomes less distinct with maturity. One black
spot is on the forehead, and it looks like an eyebrow. The
black spot is the same characteristic found in
A. xanthopunctatus and *A. trimaculatus*. The distribution
is wide, but *A. griffisi* collected for the aquarium trade
come from the Christmas Island located south from
Hawaii. *Apolemichthys griffisi* occurs at depths in excess
of 40m, and the number of this species there is not large.
Therefore *A. griffisi* is one of the more expensive fish in
the aquarium hobby. The maximum size is 25 cm.

Distribution: Christmas Island, Middle Pacific, North
Indonesia, and Papua New Guinea

The mouth of an adult turns to light purple.

This individual is a very unusual color morph.

The size of this juvenile is 3 cm. The body color of juveniles is almost the same as adults.

Apolemichthys xanthopunctatus Burgess 1974
Goldflake Angelfish, Goldspotted Angelfish,
Goldspangled Angelfish

The distribution of *Apolemichthys xanthopunctatus* is about the same as for *A. griffisi*. Juveniles of *A. xanthopunctatus* are not easy to distinguish from juveniles of *A. trimaculatus*. The only difference is in the black eye band, which passes through the eye in *A. xanthopunctatus*, but stops on the eye in *A. trimaculatus*. Juveniles are yellowish until a size of 3cm, and then the color changes quickly. The anal fin, the dorsal fin, and the caudal fin turn black, and the body develops an olive color at a size of about 5cm. Some specimens that come from Christmas Island are still yellow when the size is over 5cm. Some individuals that are yellowish compared with others may be hybrids with *A. trimaculatus*. Comparing some individuals, the number of gold flakes varies. Some individuals have a high density and a lot of gold flakes. Some individuals have only countable gold flakes. The Goldflake Angelfish usually arrives in a very good condition, and it is easy to keep. The blue mouth turns vivid when it is kept in a good quality aquarium, and it has an unbelievable beauty. Maximum size is 25 cm.

Distribution: Christmas Island, Gilbert Islands, Phoenix Islands, and Line Islands

This adult with a noble body came from Christmas Island. The size is 15cm.

The size of this juvenile that has the beginning appearance of adult characteristics is 5cm.

The size of this juvenile is 2.5 cm. The yellow body color of a small juvenile looks like *A. trimaculatus*.

These 2 individuals may be hybrids of *A xanthopunctatus* with *A. trimaculatus*. Their body color is more yellow than normal. Of course *A. trimaculatus* occurs at Christmas Island.

Apolemichthys guezei (Randall & Mauge 1978)
Reunion Angelfish

Since the time that *Apolemichthys guezei* was described in 1978, much about the species still remains mysterious. A total of ten specimens including the holotype of *A. guezei* were collected at Reunion Island in the West Indian Ocean in the early 1970's. After that there has been just one other reported sighting of *A. guezei*, recently, and just one picture was taken. The body color is dark brown, and an area from the mouth to the forehead is dark brown, possibly with a light purple hue. There are small gold spots on the body side, much like the pattern in *A. xanthopunctatus*. The soft dorsal and anal fins are rounded but more elongate than in other *Apolemichthys* spp., forming a continuous outline with the tail and giving the Reunion Angelfish an appearance reminiscent of a *Centropyge* sp. The Reunion Angelfish occurs at depths in excess of 50m, which makes it difficult to photograph or collect. It is a dream fish for aquarium hobbyists who appreciate rare angelfish. The maximum size is 15 cm.

Distribution: Known only from Reunion Island

Apolemichthys guezei photographed by John E. Randall.

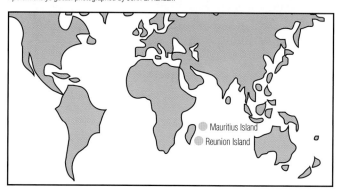

Mauritius Island
Reunion Island

Apolemichthys kingi Heemstra 1984
Tiger Angelfish

The Tiger Angelfish is named for the pattern of stripes on the dorsal part. A black spot next to the gill and a blue mouth show its close relation to *A. trimaculatus*. It is endemic to South Africa, and is common on an offshore rocky reef called "Aliwal shoal," a famous point for divers. Aliwal shoal receives a strong current that flows from Kenya to the South Pole along the east African coast. Aliwal shoal looks like a strong boat in a rapid stream, and is a very challenging place for diving. Hard coral is scattered on brown algae-covered rock, and *A. kingi* is observed at depths from 15m to 20m on any dive, nipping at the many varieties of algae growing on the rocks. Usually specimens occur singly, in cracks between rocks or under ledges. The Tiger Angelfish is shy in aquariums, and prefers to eat vegetable based foods. It should be maintained with cooler temperatures, up to 25 °C. Juveniles are not often observed because they live at a deeper depth than adults. Juveniles have white heads and a black eye band. The color pattern on the dorsal area is rough, and there is a characteristic single large eyespot on the soft dorsal fin. The color pattern on the dorsal area becomes more defined as the fish grows. The head on old adults turns to black. The size of mature adults is up to 20cm.

Distribution: Durban in the Republic of South Africa

The pattern on the dorsal part is the most beautiful in this period. The size is 13cm.

The mouth of an adult turns to light blue.

Apolemichthys kingi is very shy at Aliwal shoal. T. Nakamura (volvox)

Genus *Chaetodontoplus*

The genus *Chaetodontoplus* is a small group that occurs in the West Pacific Ocean north to Izu, in Japan, Southeast Asia, West and North Australia, and on the Great Barrier Reef. The top of the head to dorsal area is raised sharply, and the body shape is square or trapezoid, with rounded soft dorsal and anal fins. *Chaetodontoplus* spp. are both less aggressive and some species are less shy compared with other angelfishes. While the genus *Apolemichthys* seems like a division of *Holocanthus*, in a similar way *Chaetodontoplus* seems to be close to *Pomacanthus*. *Chaetodontoplus* spp. are delicate. Wild-caught adults don't adapt well to captivity, and often fail to eat in aquariums. Keeping juveniles however offers a good result.

Chaetodontoplus septentrionalis
(Temminck & Schlegel 1844)
Bluestriped Angelfish

Chaetodontoplus septentrionalis occurs at limited areas in Japan north to Izu, Taiwan, and Vietnam, while *Chaetodontoplus chrysocephalus, C. Melanosoma,* and *C. caeruleopunctatus* occur between these areas. These Angelfishes live in different areas from the East China Sea to Southeast Asia, and the distribution map showing the divisions between these *Chaetodontoplus* spp.is complicated. *Chaetodontoplus septentrionalis* is observed on rocky reefs in Honshu in the Temperate Zone all the year round. It is also found in Taiwan and Vietnam, which are tropical. The blue lines are characteristic. Sometimes individuals with irregular blue lines are found. The Bluestriped angelfish has a unique behavior of forming small groups of up to 10 individuals. Such groups are often observed at Izu. Juveniles hide around rocks in shallow water in bays at wharfs. The juveniles of the above-mentioned *Chaetodontoplus* spp. look the same. They have a black body and a yellow line on the gill covers. Juveniles have the same color on the caudal fins as the adults, either all-yellow or with a yellow edge. The maximum size of *Chaetodontoplus septentrionalis* is 22 cm.

Distribution: South Japan, Malay peninsula, Taiwan, and Vietnam

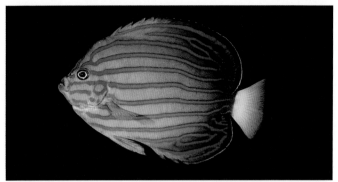

This individual with well-ordered lines came from Wakayama in Japan. The size is 13cm.

This individual with a net pattern on the head came from Vietnam. The size is 18cm.

This individual that is called "Blue Face" came from Vietnam. The size is 16cm.

This juvenile came from Izu Peninsula in Japan. The size is 2.5cm.

Chaetodontoplus chrysocephalus Bleeker 1854
Orangeface angelfish

Chaetodontoplus chrysocephalus was described in 1854.
Some ichthyologists argue this species is a hybrid.
Recently their hybrid theory was supported. Near Honshu
in Japan, especially Izu and Shikoku are places where one
can observe them often. However a group or pair has
never been found. The color pattern and color are not the
same in each individual. The individuals have few shared
characteristics. From these reasons, the hybrid theory
gains support. Now another question comes up. Which
species are the parents of *C. chrysocephalus*? One of them
must be *C. septentrionalis* because most *C. chrysocephalus*
have blue lines on the body. *Chaetodontoplus
melanosoma* or *C. caeruleopunctatus* are expected based
on the distribution and *C. chrysocephalus'* body color.
Chaetodontoplus melanosoma has a high possibility
because it is found at Izu. *Chaetodontoplus
caeruleopunctatus* occurs only in the Philippines, but the
fertilized eggs may come to Japan by prevailing currents.
It is one hypothesis with less possibility. Sometimes
C. chrysocephalus has many small blue spots on the body
like *C. caeruleopunctatus*, so still the hypothesis cannot
be abandoned. It is likely that all three species are
involved in the hybrid known as *C. chrysocephalus*, and
that the offspring are fertile and can reproduce with each
other or any of the parent species. Such a group of closely
related species is known as a syngameon. Sometimes such
populations form and then lose contact over time due to
change of sea level, but traces of their connection remain.
Perhaps the secret will be solved in the future by DNA
analysis. Debelius, Tanaka, and Kuiter (2003) suggest that
the name *C. cephaloreticulatus* should be used for the
species called *C. chrysocephalus* in this book, and that the
species shown in this book as *C. caeruleopunctatus*
should be called *C. chrysocephalus*. Observations of
C. caeruleopunctatus from the Philippines do not support
this. The maximum size of the species here called
C. chrysocephalus is 22 cm.

Distribution: Izu and Shikoku in Japan, Taiwan, and
Southeast Asia

Individual at Izu Peninsula in Japan with *C. caeruleopunctatus* spotting. The size is 20cm. N. Hashimoto

This individual at Koshiki Island in Japan has an impression of *C. melanosoma*. The size is 16cm. T. Nakamura (volvox)

This individual came from Wakayama in Japan. The size is 15 cm.

Chaetodontoplus melanosoma (Bleeker 1853)
Black velvet Angelfish

The Japanese name for *Chaetodontoplus melanosoma*, "Kiheli" means it has yellow edges on the dorsal, caudal, and anal fin. A regional variety with a completely yellow caudal fin comes from Indonesia. The body color of juveniles is black. When the body size is over 4cm, the dorsal part turns gray. Mature males have a yellow pattern on the head. *Chaetodontoplus* spp. have small scales with a velvety smoothness compared to other angelfishes. *Chaetodontoplus melanosoma*, *C. caeruleopunctatus*, and *C. meredithi* have simple colors, but their smooth skins give a unique impression. *Chaetodontoplus melanosoma* is collected from Indonesia and the Philippines regularly, and is a popular angelfish for marine aquariums. It is shy, so it should not be kept with large aggressive angelfishes in aquariums. The maximum size is 20 cm.

Distribution: North to Izu in the Western Pacific Ocean, Southeast Asia, Indonesia, and Papua New Guinea

Note: What appears to be a regional variant of *C. melanosoma* in Papua New Guinea has been described recently as a distinct species, *C. vanderloosi*. It has a black body and a pale grey area only on the face, not extending along the dorsal area.

This individual came from the Philippines. The size is 12cm.

This individual came from the Philippines. The size is 5cm.

This individual came from the Philippines. The size is 3cm.

Chaetodontoplus caeruleopunctatus
Yasuda & Tominaga 1976
Bluespotted Angelfish

Chaetodontoplus caeruleopunctatus occurs in a very
limited area that is the smallest for *Chaetodontoplus* spp.,
It only occurs in the Philippines. Juveniles look like
C. melanosoma. One distinguishing point is a yellow
caudal fin. Some juveniles of *C. melanosoma* also have a
yellow caudal fin, so positive identification of the species
requires growth to the adult phase. Growth of angelfish
juveniles, wrasse juveniles, and basslet juveniles in
aquariums is sometimes a way to know an unknown
species. Therefore, aquarium hobby knowledge and
technique are indispensable to ichthyology research. Just a
100L aquarium is enough to observe a juvenile
C. caeruleopunctatus grow. Angelfish juveniles need a lot
of food to maintain their body weight. Too little food
makes them skinny easily. The Bluespotted Angelfish is
not easy to feed. It is important to make the fish feel
secure with simple hiding shelters, and offer food such as
chopped shrimp or clam, a little at a time. The maximum
size is 14 cm.

Distribution: Philippines

This 12cm individual is the adult size.

This individual has incomplete blue spots. The size is 5cm.

The juvenile body color is close to *C. melanosoma*. The size is 2cm.

73

Chaetodontoplus duboulayi (Günther 1867)
Scribbled Angelfish

Chaetodontoplus duboulayi is one of the representative angelfishes of Australia. The Scribbled Angel changes its body colors by sex, unusual for *Chaetodontoplus* spp. Juveniles have black bodies and one yellow line, as do all *Chaetodontoplus* spp. The color change occurs at a very early stage, the body turning blue at a size of just 3 cm. The scribbled pattern appears on the body side. One yellow band from the dorsal part to the caudal fin appears in young adults, and the scribbled pattern becomes bright and clear during this period. The body shape is round, and the face becomes kind. After the sex change to males, the color pattern turns to lines, and the body shape becomes square. The change makes it easy to distinguish between males and females. The Scribbled Angelfish also has regional color morphs. In East Australia it has a yellow band, while in West Australia, the Indian Ocean side, it has a strong orange band. The maximum size is 28cm.

Distribution: From North West to North East Australia, Aru Island in Indonesia, and southern Papua New Guinea

This 25cm male is a full size adult.

The female has a round body. The size is 12cm.

The juvenile does not have a yellow band on the dorsal area. The size is 3cm.

Chaetodontoplus meredithi Kuiter 1990
Queensland Yellowtail Angelfish

In 1990, *Chaetodontoplus meredithi* was described as a distinct species from *Chaetodontoplus personifer*. *Chaetodontoplus meredithi* lives in East Australia; *C. personifer* lives in West Australia. The color of the caudal fin is a distinguishing point between these 2 species. *C. meredithi* has a yellow caudal fin. However, as we already mentioned, *C. melanosoma* in Indonesia also has a yellow-tailed regional morph. DNA analysis may demonstrate whether these are really distinct species or color morphs only. Both species have smooth black body surfaces. The head turns bluish purple with growth, and gives a special atmosphere. The face in mature males that are over 20 cm becomes blue with many yellow spots. The maximum size of males is 25 cm. *Chaetodontoplus meredithi* should be kept in quiet conditions (without aggressive tankmates) because it is sensitive.

Distribution: North East Australia

Yellow spots appear on the adult's face. The size is 25cm.

The young adult has a purple face. The size is 10cm.

The juvenile has a color similar to *C. septentrionalis*. The size is 3.5cm.

Chaetodontoplus personifer (McCulloch 1914)
Yellowtail Angelfish, Western Yellowtail Angelfish

Chaetodontoplus personifer and *C. meredithi* were confused for a long time. In *C. personifer* adults the black color of the body covers 2/3 of the caudal fin. Other color patterns are essentially the same as for *C. meredithi* from East Australia. The juveniles are identical. The maximum size of adults, however, is 35 cm for *C. personifer*, which is 10 cm larger than for *C. meredithi*. The adult males have more elongate bodies compared to females, which are more compact and rounded. As with other members of the genus, it is recommended to choose juveniles for aquarium specimens, as they adapt well compared to wild-caught adults or subadults. The diet should include vegetable matter, and there should be plenty of hiding places to make them feel comfortable.

Distribution: West Australia

The male's pattern appears slightly on this sub-adult's face. The size is 24cm.

The female's pattern appears rather like *C. meredithi*.

Chaetodontoplus niger Chan 1969
Black angelfish

Chaetodontoplus niger is almost unknown. It is a nearly all-black fish, except for the large white pectoral fins and a yellow tail. The eyes are exceptionally large for the body size. Probably because of its dark color, only a few individuals have been observed underwater. It has been sighted only at Izu, Shikoku, and Kumezima in Japan. Sometimes *C. niger* is caught by fishermen's set nets on Wakayama. Only juveniles are observed near coasts. These juveniles are less than 5 cm according to witnesses. The shallowest depth where *C. niger* has been observed is 15 m at Izu, but usually it is sighted at depths in excess of 40m. The holotype of *C. niger* was collected between Vietnam and the Philippines. Therefore it must have a fairly widespread distribution. Nothing is known about its aquarium requirements. The maximum size is unknown.

Distribution: Coast of Japan, South China Sea, and the Philippines

A sighting of this mysterious fish at East Izu Peninsula in Japan. The size is 3cm. K.Togashi

Chaetodontoplus mesoleucus (Bloch 1787)
Vermiculated angelfish

Chaetodontoplus mesoleucus is a small species occurring inside coral rich reefs. It hides in staghorn and whorled leaf corals, and with a dark line through the eye it looks like one of the many butterflyfish (*Chaetodon* spp.) that feed on hard coral. *Chaetodontoplus mesoleucus* is solitary, and has a territory around corals. The mouth and the size of the body are small in angelfishes. The mouth is useful to eat polyps and coral tissues, sponges, and algae. The beautiful color pattern looks like crêpe paper. The caudal fin is yellow, but some individuals from a part of Indonesia have a semitransparent or white caudal fin. This regional difference of appearance in caudal fins is special for *Chaetodontoplus* spp. *Chaetodontoplus mesoleucus* is one of the more popular marine aquarium fishes collected from the Philippines and Indonesia. Compared with other angelfishes, however, *C. mesoleucus* is delicate and not easy to keep in an aquarium. Do not keep with large aggressive fishes, making a quiet condition is the best way. Feeding *C. mesoleucus* is difficult without a quiet condition. Live Brine shrimp, *Mysis*, and copepods are good choices for tempting fishes that do not eat well. The maximum size is 18 cm, though typical adult specimens are only 10 cm.

Distribution: North to Okinawa in Western Pacific Ocean, Philippines, Indonesia, Malaysia, Solomon Islands, and Papua New Guinea

This individual with a blue mouth came from Indonesia. The size is 6cm.

This individual has a translucent tail. The size is 4cm.

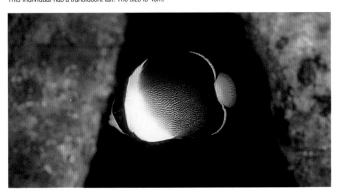

The juvenile has the same body color as adults. The size is 2cm.

Chaetodontoplus ballinae Whitley 1959
Ballina Angelfish

Chaetodontoplus ballinae was discovered at Ballina in New South Wales, Australia in 1959. The habits of this species are almost unknown. It is believed that *C. ballinae* normally occurs at depths in excess of 70m. After the first individual was found, no more were seen or caught for a long time. The next individual was found at a small atoll near Lord Howe Island in the State of New South Wales. Actually, *C. ballinae* is not known to occur at Lord Howe Island. An atoll called Balls pyramid that is 23 km from Lord Howe Island, is the only known place to see *C. ballinae*. The site is a rock mountain in the ocean and is one of the many diving points in the area. Many fishes gather around this rock mountain. The Ballina Angelfish occurs at depth of from 20 to 25m there. Some corals are found, and the view underwater looks like a subtropical zone. *Chaetodontoplus ballinae* occurs singly or as pairs, and they do not run away from divers. Because *C. ballinae* is not accustomed to seeing divers, it has no fear of them. *Chaetodontoplus conspicillatus, Genicanthus semicinctus,* and *Centropyge tibicen* are found in the same area, but juveniles of *C. ballinae* have not been seen. The juveniles may occur deeper than adults, or they may live in zones with very strong currents, where divers are unlikely to go. The Ballina Angelfish is not available in the aquarium trade because Lord Howe Island and nearby areas are protected as a World Heritage site. Also, since adult sized *Chaetodontoplus* do not adapt well to aquariums, the juveniles must be found for any appropriate attempt to maintain the species in captivity. The maximum size is not known, but should be at least 25 cm.

Distribution: New South Wales in Australia, and Lord Howe Island

A wonderful sight 20m deep at Balls Pyramid, near Lord Howe Island. T.Nakamura (volvox)

Usually a pair of adults is observed. T. Nakamura (volvox)

Mts. Lidgbird and Gower at Lord Howe Island. The coral reefs are inside the bay. T. Nakamura (volvox)

Chaetodontoplus conspicillatus (Waite,1900)
Conspicuous Angelfish

Chaetodontoplus conspicillatus has a unique color pattern for any angelfish. Juveniles smaller than 4 cm are dark black, the same as juveniles of other *Chaetodontoplus* spp. The color changes dramatically with growth. The dorsal part turns to gray, and the edge is bordered by a wide bluish white margin when the size of juveniles is just 5 cm. However the face color changes more slowly. In juveniles over 10cm the face begins to turn orange. The face becomes striking when *C conspicillatus* attains a size of 15cm. It is a vivid orange with a pair of blue rings that look like eyeglasses, and blue borders on the gill covers. The vivid orange and blue faces of males are beautiful. Females have a round body, and males have a long body. The Conspicuous angelfish is very popular in aquariums, but it is one of the most expensive angelfishes. Most come from New Caledonia, which is not one of the traditional collection regions for aquarium fishes, so they are not often available. If *C. conspicillatus* becomes one of your aquarium fishes, make sure that there are no other big or aggressive angelfishes in the aquarium. It must feel secure to begin feeding, and prefers to be the dominant fish in the aquarium. The maximum size is about 25 cm, though it is often reported to be only half this size.

Distribution: Southeast Australia, Lord Howe Island, Norfolk Island, and New Caledonia

This 25cm male is a full sized adult.

This young individual has a light orange face. The size is 6cm.

This hybrid with *C. meredithi* came from the Great Barrier Reef. The size is 8cm.

Beauty, intellect and sweetness.

The size of this juvenile is 3cm.

Aberrant color morph from the Maldives.
There is no black pigment.
The size of this individual is 16 cm.

Genus *Pygoplites*

The genus *Pygoplites* has only one species, *Pygoplites diacanthus*. This angelfish has a gentle face with a sharply pointed mouth. This species shares many characteristics with *Holacanthus* spp. However, it is interesting that the secretive juveniles, which live in caves, are quite similar in appearance and bahavior to *Centropyge* spp. In the Pacific Ocean these juveniles often share caves with *Paracentropyge multifasciata*, which seems to mimic them. In both species the juveniles have a blue ocellus (eye spot) on the soft dorsal fin.

Pygoplites diacanthus (Boddaert 1772)
Regal Angelfish

Pygoplites diacanthus is a colorfully striped angelfish that occurs widely on coral reefs from the Pacific Ocean to the Indian Ocean and Red Sea. With its small mouth and eyes concealed behind a dark blue-edged band one gets the impression it has a tender, sweet disposition. In fact, *P. diacanthus* is gentle and sensitive. The Regal Angelfish lives in coral-rich complicated reef structures at depths from a few meters to over 20 m. Juveniles are common only in caves or crevices. Adults in the Pacific Ocean are also most common around caves, are very shy, but sometimes venture out among corals growing on horizontal bottom. In the Red Sea the adults are much bolder, and are commonly seen on horizontal reef substrates. The color morph of *P. diacanthus* depends on the region where it is from. Indian Ocean and Red Sea specimens are distinct from the Pacific Ocean form. The basic color patterns are the same in these color morphs, but individuals from the Pacific Ocean are less vivid, and have a gray or bluish face. Though small juveniles from the Pacific Ocean may be brilliant orange, individuals from the Indian Ocean are more vivid at all sizes, and have a yellowish or orange face as adults. The Red Sea morph is also substantially bolder in aquariums, and its behavior is markedly different. In the Pacific Ocean form, juveniles are skittish, and flit their fins like a *Centropyge* sp. The adults retain the skittish trait and often fail to eat in captivity. The Indian Ocean and especially the Red Sea form swim with a much smoother, relaxed, and confident manner, like a *Pomacanthus* sp. They also usually feed readily on all kinds of food. They should be offered various seaweeds to maintain their bright coloration and health. The maximum size is 25 cm.

Distribution: West Pacific Ocean, Micronesia, New Caledonia, Indonesia, Central and west Indian Ocean, and Red Sea

Adults from the Red Sea and Indian Ocean have yellow/orange faces.

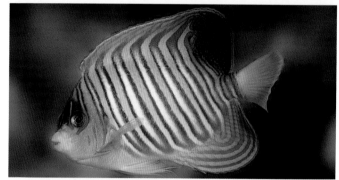

This individual came from the Philippines. The size is 14cm.

This individual came from the Maldives. The size is 2.5cm.

This juvenile came from the Maldives. The size is 2cm.

This juvenile came from the Philippines. The size is 3.5cm.

This individual with aberrant color came from the Maldives.

Aberrant individual from the Pacific Ocean.

Pomacanthus imperator from Vietnam. The Pacific Ocean morph has a filament on the dorsal fin and a yellow tail.

Pomacanthus imperator from the Red Sea. The Red Sea and Indian Ocean morph does not have a filament. The tail is orange.

Genus *Pomacanthus*

The genus *Pomacanthus* consists of boldly colored angelfish that, like the genus *Holacanthus,* grow to a large size. Since they will outgrow an average sized aquarium, one must consider this eventuality, and plan to provide a larger home for them. Adults that have grown up from juveniles in a small aquarium are nevertheless comfortable despite the lack of space. As with other angelfish genera, the color and pattern on *Pomacanthus* spp. juveniles differs from adults, and it changes with growth. The transition to adult coloration is amazing to observe and is a unique, charming feature in each species of *Pomacanthus.* The juveniles of many *Pomacanthus* species share common patterns and are very similarly colored, while the adults have very distinct appearance. The genus is divided into three subgenera (*Pomacanthus, Euxiphipops,* and *Pomacanthodes*) based on distinctive physical shape. Members of the subgenus *Euxiphipops.* have a body shape that is stretched out, with wider soft dorsal and anal fins, and elongate ventral fins. *Euxiphipops* does not have a wide distribution. It occurs in South East Asia mainly. Usually a swimming pair is found in *Euxiphipops species,* while other *Pomacanthus* spp. adults occur in groups or pairs. While *Holacanthus* and *Pomacanthus* are similar by virtue of their large size, there are distinct differences between them based on the architecture of the mouth. In *Holacanthus* the upper lip is equal in size or larger than the lower lip, while in *Pomacanthus* the lower lip is larger and angled upward, giving the face a "tough" expression.

Pomacanthus imperator (Bloch 1787)
Emperor Angelfish

Pomacanthus imperator is the most familiar angelfish to aquarists and divers. Juveniles are called "Uzumaki," which means whirl in Japan, referring to the circular pattern on the body. The time of color change to the adult pattern depends on the individual. The shape of the soft dorsal fin differs depending on where *P. imperator* comes from. Individuals from the Pacific Ocean have a long dorsal filament, while those from the Indian Ocean and Red Sea have a rounded soft dorsal fin, without filaments. However *P. imperator* with a round shaped dorsal fin is reported around the Christmas Islands in the Pacific Ocean. *Pomacanthus imperator* is referred to as the king of angelfish. Adults swim with a manner of ease as if they were the king of reef. Big adults guard their territories aggressively, and make a loud sound "Guo Guo" with their mouth. On the other hand, juveniles swim in a meandering manner. Smaller than 5cm juveniles are cleaner fishes that pick parasites from the skin of big fishes. In aquariums it is normal to see the Emperor angelfish turn sideways slowly. They have a sweet inquisitive disposition. They feed on all kinds of food offered, but must eat a substantial amount of vegetable matter to remain healthy and colorful. The maximum size is 40 cm.

Distribution: North to Izu islands in the west Pacific Ocean, Middle Pacific Ocean as far east as Hawaii (rarely), Great Barrier Reef, New Caledonia, Austral Islands, Middle and west Indian Ocean, and Red Sea

This individual was observed at Christmas Island in the of Republic of Kiribati. The size is 22cm. T.Nakamura(volvox)

The body color and pattern of this individual is changing to an adult.

The juvenile color pattern sometimes remains even though the size is over 10cm.

The size of this juvenile is 3cm.

Pomacanthus semicirculatus (Cuvier 1831)
Koran Angelfish, Semicircle Angelfish

Pomacanthus semicirculatus also has a wide distribution like *P. imperator*. Sometimes *P. semicirculatus* juveniles can be collected near Tokyo. Unfortunately these individuals are dead by winter due to the cold temperature of the water. Near Hachijo Island, big adults are observed often because a warm current comes there. In the west part of Japan, at Wakayama and Shikoku is the same situation, and some of them survive during winter. Like *P. imperator*, *P. semicirculatus* also has regional color morphs. Individuals from East Africa have the color pattern of juveniles even at a size of 15cm. Juveniles from the Pacific Ocean start to turn to white on ventral parts at about 10cm. The background body color on adults from the Indian Ocean turns green. The metallic blue border on the body on adults from the Indian Ocean is more vivid than on individuals from the Pacific Ocean. Adults from the Pacific Ocean have a chic background color, and the mouth is yellowish. *Pomacanthus semicirculatus* is easy to keep in an aquarium, so it is one of the best angelfishes for beginners. The maximum size is 40 cm.

Distribution: West Pacific Ocean, including west and East Australia and Lord Howe Island, north to southern Japan, Middle Pacific Ocean to Samoa, and Indian Ocean

This individual is a nice looking adult. The size is 30cm.

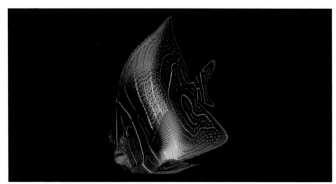

This individual starting to change the body color came from the Philippines. The size is 16cm.

This individual came from East Africa. The size is 18cm.

This individual came from the Philippines. The size is 3cm.

Pomacanthus sexstriatus (Cuvier 1831)
Sixbanded Angelfish, Sixbar Angelfish

Pomacanthus sexstriatus is called the "Sixbanded angelfish" based on the six dark, wide vertical bands on the body. This beautiful angelfish has blue spots on each scale. The color pattern of juveniles is nearly the same as that of *P. semicirculatus* and *P. chrysurus*, and distinguishing them is difficult at first glance. The white lines are glassy on *P. sexstriatus*, and wide lines alternate with narrow ones. In *P. chrysurus* the lines are almost all the same width. Juveniles of *P. sexstriatus* have a tail with a design pattern on it until a size of 5cm. The tail of *P. chrysurus* quickly turns yellow. That is why juveniles larger than 5cm are easy to distinguish. *Pomacanthus sexstriatus* is one of the largest species in the genus *Pomacanthus*. The maximum size is 50cm. The subgenus *Euxiphipops* to which *P. sexstriatus* belongs also contains *P. navarchus* and *P. xanthometopon*. Hybrids within *Euxiphipops* are reported, for example *P. sexstriatus* x *P. xanthometopon*, and *P. xanthometopon* x *P. navarchus*.

Distribution: Ryukyu Islands, South East Asia to Malaysia, Australia, New Caledonia, Solomon Islands, Indonesia

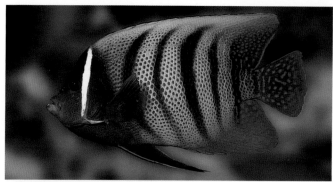

This adult came from Vietnam. The size is 30cm.

The center of the body is a pale in this older juvenile. The size is 8cm.

The body color of juveniles is similar to other *Pomacanthus* spp. The size is 3.5cm.

Pomacanthus navarchus (Cuvier 1831)
Majestic Angelfish, Blue Girdled Angelfish

The combination of blue, purple, and orange in the adult Majestic Angelfish is unforgettable. Juveniles have 8 or 9 narrow blue lines. The color change to adults is very quick, and 3cm juveniles have an orange area near the dorsal fin. Some individuals already have adult body colors even though their body sizes are only 5cm. The maximum size for *P. navarchus* is 25cm, small for the subgenus *Euxiphipops*. Juveniles and adults occur in rich coral lagoons or outside on the coral rich reef edge. *Pomacanthus navarchus* is less aggressive than other angelfishes, and has strong cautiousness. It hides in the shadows or under the corals whenever it sees divers or large fishes. Juveniles are especially hard to find underwater because they always live in rock shadows or under coral heads. Small individuals are more shy than larger ones. They are delicate fishes and are difficult to keep in aquariums. Wild-caught adults sometimes fail to eat. Adults have large ventral fins, and the orange color is more intense.

Distribution: Philippines, Indonesia, Micronesia including Palau and Yap, Solomon Islands, and Papua New Guinea

This adult came from the Philippines. The size is 22cm.

This individual with a long ventral fin is just 10cm long.

This unusual color morph came from Indonesia.

The size of this juvenile is 3cm.

Pomacanthus xanthometopon (Bleeker 1853)
Blueface angelfish

Pomacanthus xanthometopon juveniles have a color pattern of vertical white lines on a blue background that is more or less the same as other juveniles of *Pomacanthus* spp. *P. xanthometopon* turns to adult color quickly compared with other angelfishes. The color change starts from a body size of 5 cm. First the face around eyes turns orange. Next, a cream-colored area spreads from the dorsal area downward, and the white lines disappear. Some individuals have the adult color by just 7 or 8 cm. *Pomacanthus xanthometopon* has some regional color morphs. Individuals from the Pacific Ocean have a yellow area around eye and ventral parts. Individuals from the Maldives and Indian Ocean have more vivid orange color on the same area. Some individuals have one big black spot on the dorsal fin, and others do not. The reason for the existence of the black spot is still unknown. The orange or red color loses brilliance easily in aquariums. To keep this color brilliant, good water quality and good nutrition are important. Keeping angelfishes in aquariums is easy, but keeping the color the same as in nature requires effort. The maximum size is 38 cm.

Distribution: North to Ryukyu Islands in the western Pacific Ocean, Philippines, Indonesia, Micronesia, Great Barrier Reef, Sri Lanka, and the Maldives

This individual came from the Maldives. The size is 26cm.

This individual came from the Philippines. The size is 12cm.

The white lines on the body of this juvenile are indented. The size is 6cm.

Pomacanthus maculosus (Forsskal 1775)
Yellowbar angelfish

Pomacanthus maculosus is a representative angelfish from the Red Sea and East Africa. A large yellow mark appears on the side. The shape of the yellow mark varies. Juveniles have the typical color found in other *Pomacanthus* spp. The narrow lines and a yellow tail are distinguishing points. The color change is different by individuals. Individuals from the Red Sea, Persian Gulf and Gulf of Oman develop adult coloration more quickly than individuals from the East coast of Africa. Individuals from the East coast of Africa have a juvenile coloration even though the size is already 10 cm. However the adult colors are not different, just the rate of color change. The body color of adults changes slightly depend on environmental conditions. Strong lighting and good quality water make a blue body with a vivid yellow tail and crescent. Under the dim light, the body color becomes gray. This species is one of the toughest angelfishes. Keeping *P. maculosus* in aquariums is easy. The adults grow up to 50 cm in nature, but the size would be less than 30 cm in typical sized aquariums.

Distribution: Red Sea, Gulf of Oman, and East coast of Africa

This individual came from the Red Sea. The size is 30cm.

This individual came from Kenya. The size is 15cm.

This hybrid with *P. semicirculatus* came from Kenya.

This juvenile came from Kenya. The size is 3cm.

Juvenile *P. maculosus* from East Africa. The size is 5cm.

Pomacanthus asfur (Forsskal 1775)
Arabian Angelfish, Crescent Angelfish, Asfur Angelfish

Pomacanthus asfur has a moon shape design on the side. The pattern and color are similar to *P. maculosus*, but the body of *P. asfur* is darker and the yellow mark is more clearly defined. The scales are a vivid deep purplish blue that has to be viewed in bright light to appreciate, since it otherwise blends with the black background. Additionally, juveniles of *P. asfur* have more blue bands, and the yellow mark appears quickly. Juveniles change to adult coloring completely at a size of 7 or 8cm. There is some regional variation in the yellow mark. It is short and small on individuals from the Gulf of Aquaba in the interior of the Red Sea. The yellow mark is large, and sometimes reaches the ventral part on individuals from the Gulf of Aden. Compared with the bold *P. maculosus*, *P. asfur* is more cautious, so it is always hiding when kept with other angelfish. If you want to keep it with other angelfishes, you should introduce *P. asfur* first, or choose a big one. The size of adults is typically 25 cm, but they are reported to reach 40 cm. The dorsal fin and anal fin have a very long filament, sometimes as long as the rest of the body.

Distribution: Red Sea and Gulf of Aden, and the East African coast as far south as Zanzibar

The filaments on the dorsal and anal fins are very long. The size is 20cm.

The yellow pattern starts to appear. The size is 3.5cm.

The juvenile is bluer than *P. maculosus.* The size is 2.5cm.

This color morph has a white band. The size is 10cm.

Pomacanthus annularis (Bloch 1787)
Bluering Angelfish, White Tail Angelfish, Annularis Angelfish

The sweep of curved concentric blue lines from the gill cover to the dorsal fin in the adult *Pomacanthus annularis* is impressive. A conspicuous circle on the gill cover is the source of the common name, though another name is sometimes used, "White Tail Angelfish," referring to the tail of adults. Juveniles have the most brilliant blue lines in *Pomacanthus* spp. The color change is odd. Juveniles lose the blue color, and the body turns brown as the pattern of juveniles and adults is displayed at the same time. The color is so amazing. All *Pomacanthus* spp. have this period of color change, and it is fascinating to witness. Adults develop a filament on the soft dorsal fin, while the anal fin is curved. In captivity large adults develop side branches on the curved blue lines, forming an ever changing pattern. Keeping *P. annularis* is not difficult, the same as other hardy *Pomacanthus* spp. It is important to feed often, and include large amounts of vegetable based foods. The maximum size is 45 cm.

Distribution: East Africa, Southeast Asia to southern Japan, Indonesia, Papua New Guinea, New Caledonia

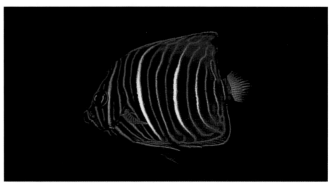

The size of this juvenile is 3.5cm.

This individual has begun to change to adult body color. The size is 6cm.

The attractive adult is massive. The size is 35cm.

Pomacanthus rhomboides (Gilchrist & Thompson, 1908)
Old woman Angelfish

The Old woman Angelfish is an unusual species, and hard to find in the aquarium trade. Most of angelfishes are colorful, but as an adult *Pomacanthus rhomboides* is not. Juveniles are similar to the juveniles of *P. annularis*, and are not easy to distinguish. The change to adult coloration is slow. The juvenile coloration disappears when the size is over 10cm. The body of adults is dull metallic blue and gray. Mature adults have a pale triangular area in front of the tail. The body shape is high, as in *P. annularis*, but when the adults spread their fins the body is almost diamond-shaped because the soft dorsal and anal fins are short. *Pomacanthus rhomboides* adults form groups of 20 or 30 individuals. The maximum body size is 46 cm.

Distribution: East coast of Africa and the Gulf of Aden at the entrance of the Red Sea. The main distribution is offshore of Durban in South Africa and Madagascar

This individual came from South Africa. The size is 4cm.

This individual was photographed in South Africa. The size is 10cm. T. Nakamura (volvox)

This individual was photographed in South Africa. The size is 25cm. T. Nakamura (volvox)

Pomacanthus chrysurus (Cuvier 1831)
Earspot Angel, Chrysurus Angelfish, Goldtail Angelfish

Pomacanthus chrysurus has a unique feature. The white lines of juveniles remain in the mature adults. Juveniles are typical of *Pomacanthus* spp. The color pattern looks like *P. sexstriatus* and especially like *P. semicirculatus*, but *P. chrysurus* has fewer prominent white vertical bands, each separated by a narrow blue vertical band. Like *P. maculosus*, juveniles of *P. chrysurus* develop yellow tails as they grow. Juveniles at a size of 10cm have yellow tails and brown heads. The brown color becomes black in adults, and there are 6 or 7 vertical white lines. The adult's tail is vivid yellow, and there are beautiful metallic blue radial lines around eyes and mouth, and bordering the gills. Adults also have a circular mark on the gill covers, hence the common name, "Earspot Angel." For the aquarium trade, *P. chrysurus* is exported from Kenya in small quantities, and they are not often available. They are hardy in captivity. The maximum size is 33 cm.

Distribution: Gulf of Aden to South Africa East Africa, Seychelles, Comoros and Madagascar

This individual came from Kenya. The size is 4.5cm.

This individual came from Kenya. The size is 10cm.

This individual came from Kenya. The size is 20cm.

This individual shows the full adult coloration. The size is 35cm.

The mystery of juvenile coloration

Why do *Pomacanthus* spp. have the same color pattern in juveniles? This *uniformity* of color and pattern may afford the similar benefits to a school uniform. They wear the same color uniform, and it conveys that they are small children. Therefore, the color pattern tells other fishes "please, we are small juveniles, so do not attack us." It is a kind of distinctive sign. Angelfishes are not migratory fishes, and all have a territory, including *Pomacanthus* spp. When an invader enters an angelfish's territory, a fight or a chase is often the result. Sometimes there is a big battle between fishes of the same size. The color pattern of blue and white bands tells others within the same or closely related species that the fishes are juveniles, and these juveniles are not involved in the battle. This way, juveniles can survive within the same territory as adults.

In addition, juveniles clean other fishes, and this habit also helps them to survive on reefs. Juveniles of *Pomacanthus imperator* swim strangely, moving the body in a meandering way. The swimming is a mimicry or convergence of the exaggerated swimming behavior of the Cleaner Wrasse, *Labroides dimidiatus*, which bobs up and down to attract attention. The strange swimming appears to convey the message that it is a cleaner fish.

Pomacanthus sextriatus

Pomacanthus xanthometopon

Pomacanthus navarchus

Pomacanthus semicirculatus

Pomacanthus maculosus

Pomacanthus maculosus

Pomacanthus semicirculatus hybrid.

Pomacanthus semicirculatus

Pomacanthus rhomboides

Pomacanthus paru (Bloch 1787)
French Angelfish

Pomacanthus paru is one of the representative angelfish of the Atlantic Ocean. *Pomacanthus paru*, *P. arcuatus*, and *P. zonipectus* are unique angelfishes that have some points of difference compared with the *Pomacanthus* spp. from the Indian and Pacific Oceans. First, the shape of body is taller. When the all the fins are spread, the body height and length are almost the same. Juveniles of these 3 species have nearly the same color, but it is not the blue and white typical color pattern of Indo-Pacific *Pomacanthus* juveniles. Instead the major bands are yellow. While these 3 species are very closely related to each other, only *P. zonipectus* is classified in the subgenus *Pomacanthodes*, which contains *P. imperator* and *P. maculosus*. The distribution of these 3 species is separated by the landmass of Central America, but they nevertheless have to be close relatives of each other. The color pattern of juveniles is the reason for the theory. Juveniles of *P. paru* and *P. arcuatus* have very similar coloration. The distinguishing point between them is the shape of the caudal fin and the yellow line on it. *Pomacanthus paru* has a yellow line across the caudal peduncle and around the edge of the entire caudal fin, which is round. *Pomacanthus arcuatus* has a yellow line across only the caudal peduncle, with a clear edge to its more squared caudal fin. *Pomacanthus arcuatus* juveniles also have a white or yellow line through the lips. When individuals grow to the size of 10cm or more, the difference between these 2 species is clearer. Then golden edged scales appear on a black body in *P. paru*. Adult French angelfish have a blue face, yellow eye shadow, white lips, white nostrils, and an orange filament on the soft dorsal fin. The adults form long-lasting pairs but sometimes spawning groups are found at dusk, often mixed with *P. arcuatus*.

Young *P. paru* from Florida, the Bahamas, and the Caribbean have an exaggerated undulating way of swimming, which advertises that they are cleaners. In juveniles from Brazil this swimming behavior is much reduced or non-existent. The maximum size is 41 cm.

Distribution: Florida, Bahamas, East cost of the USA with juveniles to New England in summer, but adults ranging to the Carolinas only, Gulf of Mexico, the Caribbean, Brazil, and Eastern Atlantic

This juvenile has 4 bands on the body. The size is 2cm.

The juvenile body color and pattern remain a long time. The size is 6cm.

The adult's and juvenile color appears on this individual. The size is 12cm.

This is the full adult coloration. P/T. Nakamura (volvox)

Pomacanthus arcuatus (Linnaeus 1758)
Gray Angelfish, Black Angelfish

While the adult *Pomacanthus paru* has many gold scales on a dark black body, *P. arcuatus* has a more subdued gray body color. Only one area on the adult *P. arcuatus* has a vivid color, just the yellow inside of the pectoral fins. The size of adults is larger than *P. paru*. The reported maximum body size is 60cm. Juveniles of *P. arcuatus* and *P. paru* behave as cleaner fishes. They pick parasites from the skin of other fishes. They share similar yellow bands, and both have a blue border on the ventral fins and a blue spot on the anal fin. Some specimens have blue on the soft dorsal fin as well. The color change to adults in *P. arcuatus* is slow, the same as for *P. paru*. With growth, the yellow lines disappear, beginning near the caudal fin. The adults have light-edged dark spots on the scales. The color and pattern of the adult *P. arcuatus* looks like *P. paru* without vivid colors. In nature, *P. arcuatus* adults form pairs. Juveniles occur in saltwater creeks or bays sometimes. The Gray Angelfish is one of the more popular aquarium fishes. Many sizes are available in the shops, and you can choose from small juveniles to adults over 20cm. They come from Florida year round. Whenever you want to have *P. arcuatus* and *P. paru* in your aquarium, you have to think about their size as adults. A large tank of from 400 to 500 L is required for keeping *P. arcuatus* and *P. paru* for their lifetime. P. arcuatus shows off its beautiful appeal whenever the aquascape layout in the aquarium is close to nature.

Distribution: The Caribbean, the Coast of Brazil, Gulf of Mexico, and the east coast of the USA, juveniles as far north as New England in summer, but adults only as far north as North Carolina

The juvenile looks a lot like *P. paru*. The size is 3cm.

The individual has almost full adult body color. T. Ikeda

Usually a pair of adults is observed. T. Nakamura (volvox)

Pomacanthus zonipectus (Gill 1862)
Cortez Angelfish

Pomacanthus zonipectus is the closest relative of *P. paru* that occurs in the Pacific Ocean. Juveniles have a black body with alternating yellow and blue lines. It is easy to distinguish *Pomacanthus zonipectus* because it has the alternating lines. *Pomacanthus zonipectus* occurs in the east Pacific Ocean now, but it may have occurred in the Caribbean a long time ago.

Based on the German scientist Alfred Lothar Wegener's theory of "continental drift", 65 million years ago the North American continent and South American continent were separate, but then plate tectonics connected them and formed two separate oceans. While the juveniles of *P. zonipectus* look like juveniles of *P. arcuatus* and *P. paru*, the color pattern on the adults is totally different. The color in *P. zonipectus* is not elegant, but it is wild. The large adults are more powerful. *P. zonipectus* occurs not just on coral reefs, but also along rugged rocks that form a common habitat within its range. It (along with *P. paru* and *P. arcuatus*) is reported to be good to eat. The maximum size is 46 cm.

Distribution: Gulf of California, Mexico, Coast of Central America to Peru, and Galapagos

The juvenile advertises its habit as a cleaner. The size is 4cm.

This individual has almost full adult body color. The size is 24cm.

The adult in nature has a bright color. T. Nakamura (volvox)

Holacanthus ciliaris from Florida.
The size is 28cm.

Holacanthus ciliaris from Brazil.
This individual has vivid blue.
The size is 20cm.

Genus *Holacanthus*

The members of the genus *Holacanthus* grow to a large size, and, with only one exception, have juvenile coloration that changes substantially as they mature. The upper lip is positioned a little forward of the lower. Formation of pairs of adults is sometimes observed, but some species form harems, one male with several females, or large groups. Some species are very aggressive, and this should be considered when planning an aquarium for them.

Holacanthus spp. in East Pacific Ocean are classified into a subgenus, *Plitops.* A distinguishing behavior of the subgenus *Plitops* is the formation of large groups of adults. Other *Holacanthus* spp. do not make large groups, though they may form harems. The groups are even bigger during a breeding season. During the season, smaller groups come together to make one large group, and thus many "colonies" come to one place.

Holacanthus passer and *H. clarionensis* clean the skin of stingrays and sharks even as adults. By comparison, the habit of cleaning other reef fishes is seen in several *Pomacanthus* spp. juveniles, but the adults of these cleaners lose the habit.

Holacanthus ciliaris (Linnaeus 1758)
Queen Angelfish

The Queen Angelfish is often featured as a representative of all angelfishes, and it is popular with aquarists just like the other representative angel, *Pomacanthus imperator*. Another angelfish in the East Pacific Ocean, *Holacanthus passer*, has a similar color pattern, and is called "King Angelfish" (page 101). *Holacanthus ciliaris* has a wide distribution, and regional color morphs are observed. Some color morphs may also be related to the existence of *Holacanthus bermudensis* within its range, because fertile hybrids frequently occur. Juveniles of *Holacanthus ciliaris* have short dorsal fins and anal fins, and no crown. At this stage, the juveniles have individual color patterns. Choosing a favorite one from among several juveniles is fun for aquarists. On the other hand, keeping the brilliant color and characteristic appearance from juveniles of *Holacanthus ciliaris* is difficult. The water condition, light condition and food affect the color of *Holacanthus ciliaris*. Vivid blue individuals lose the blue color, and turn yellow under poor conditions. Keeping the sensitive colors of *H. ciliaris* requires knowledge and technique for maintenance, like the reef keeping hobby. Therefore keeping *H. ciliaris* in aquariums requires effort and planning.

Distribution: Florida, Bahamas, the Caribbean, Bermuda, Coast of Brazil, and St. Paul's Rocks

This juvenile with a dark color came from Brazil. The size is 8cm.

The size of this individual is 6cm.

This young adult has a crown. The size is 13cm.

Holacanthus bermudensis Goode 1876
Blue Angelfish

Holacanthus bermudensis was described 118 years after
H. ciliaris. Why was it recognized so late? *H. bermudenisis*
looks similar to *H. ciliaris,* and furthermore they freely breed,
and the hybrids are fertile. The crown is not present on the
forehead of *H. bermudensis,* but a faint blue mark is
sometimes on the same location. The body color in adults is
light blue gray, not vivid. The edges on the tail, soft dorsal
and anal fins are yellow. While *H. ciliaris* has a completely
yellow tail, *H. bermudensis* has a pale gray or pale blue tail
with a yellow edge. Juveniles are not as easy to distinguish,
but the white vertical stripes on *H. bermudensis* are straight,
and on *H. ciliaris* they are more curved, especially the middle
one, like a "v" turned sideways. Unfortunately the hybrids
confuse the distinctions, since a range of intermediate forms
exists. *H. bermudensis* has a limited range. The hybrids occur
only in these areas. The maximum size is reported to be 45
cm, but the elongate dorsal and anal fin filaments easily make
for a total length exceeding 60 cm.

Distribution: Yucatan Mexico, Gulf of Mexico, Florida, East
coast of USA to North Carolina, Bahamas, and Bermuda

The size of this juvenile is 3.5cm.

The color changing to an adult happens quickly. The change is finished by 10cm.

A young adult *H. bermudensis* with elegant fin extensions.

103

Color morphs and hybrids of *Holacanthus ciliaris*

Hybrids between *H. ciliaris* and *H. bermudenisis* often appear. The hybrids were once called "*Holacanthus townsendi*," or in some aquarium literature there were confused descriptions that referred to the hybrid as *H. ciliaris*, and the true Queen angelfish as *H. townsendi*. These many hybrids mean that *H. ciliaris* and *H. bermudenisis* are exchanging genes. In hybrids the face has an unclear crown. The body color varies by the individual, ranging from like *H. ciliaris* to like *H. bermudensis*. The color pattern of hybrid juveniles is similar to *H. ciliaris*.

Holacanthus ciliaris from Florida. This individual is very blue. The size is 16cm.

Rare hybrid between *Holacanthus ciliaris* and *Holacanthus tricolor* collected in Palm Beach, Florida by Eric Reichardt

This adult hybrid with nearly full *H. ciliaris* coloration has long filaments. The size is 30cm.

Holacanthus ciliaris from St. Paul's Rocks.

Powder blue individual of the hybrid between *Holacanthus ciliaris* and *Holacanthus bermudenisis*.

Holacanthus ciliaris at St. Paul's Rocks.

When discussing *Holacanthus ciliaris*, St. Paul's Rocks located in the Atlantic north of Brazil is a special place to consider. *Holacanthus ciliaris* with amazing color morphs occur near these small islands. The colors and body shapes of *H. ciliaris* at St. Paul's Rocks are distinct from typical *H. ciliaris* of the Caribbean. Especially the Koi-color varieties that look like Japanese's Koi are mysterious. At St. Paul's Rocks the most similar to typical-colored Queen Angelfish individuals have vivid orange bodies. Another type has a blue body with a white tail, which is reminiscent of the Clipperton Angelfish. Usually these individuals have strangely shaped, high bodies with short filaments on the dorsal and anal fins. Such unique individuals appear commonly only at St. Paul's Rocks. The reason for these color morphs is still unknown, but one popular hypothesis is that because St. Paul's Rocks is isolated by strong currents, this increases the possibility of inter breeding. Some individuals have come to Japan. Seeing a white individual is an aquarist's dream.

Koi color *H. ciliaris* in rock reef at deep depth. O. Junior

Blue body with a white tail. O. Junior

All white body. O. Junior

Vivid orange body. O. Junior

Holacanthus tricolor (Bloch 1759)
Rock beauty

The contrast of black and yellow is impressive. Juveniles, which associate frequently with fire corals (*Millepora* spp.), have a large blue-ringed eyespot on the side that becomes a large black area with growth. The blue lines on the eyes make the face of *Holacanthus tricolor* unique, and the adults have blue "lipstick." Adult males have orange spots on the tail, and may develop tail filaments. The size of *H. tricolor* is from 25 to 30cm, smaller than other *Holacanthus* spp. Previously the collecting and handling of this species were not well develope, so the condition of imported *H. tricolor* was bad. As a result, aquarists had the idea that keeping H. tricolor is difficult. More recently the condition of imported *H. tricolor* is much better, and it is the most popular of the Caribbean Angelfishes. The distribution is the same as *Holacanthus ciliaris*. Minor regional color morphs exist. For example, individuals from Brazil have wide red bands on the outer edge of the dorsal and anal fins. The red bands appear at a size of 5 or 6cm, and remain through adulthood The important point for keeping H. tricolor well is to avoid keeping it with other large angelfishes. Sometimes *H. tricolor* becomes a target for attackers. However, if you want to keep other angelfishes, put *H. tricolor* in the tank first. After it is well established in the tank, another angelfish can be added.

Distribution: Florida, Gulf of Mexico, Bahamas, Bermuda, the Caribbean, and coast of Brazil

The juvenile has an eyespot. The size is 3.5cm.

This individual with orange bands came from Brazil.

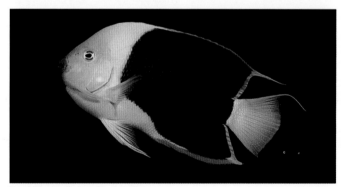

The adult has long filaments. The size is 20cm.

Holacanthus clarionensis Gilbert 1890
Clarion angelfish

The orange body of *Holacanthus clarionensis* is rare in angelfishes. Juveniles have blue vertical bands in the typical pattern seen on other *Holacanthus* spp. The main distribution of *H. clarionensis* is within the territorial waters of Mexico. The Mexican government protects this territory for animals and plants, and *H. clarionensis* may not be collected in there. Now *H. clarionensis* is collected only at Península de Baja California. Therefore *H. clarionensis* is generally not traded as an aquarium fish. Sometimes, very rarely, *H. clarionensis* is seen. Of course it is a very expensive fish. The maximum size is 20 cm.

Distribution: Lapaz, Clarion Island, Revillagigedo Islands, and Clipperton Island

This juvenile still has beautiful blue lines. The size is 4cm.

The size of this individual is 10cm.

The body color of adults is vivid, and they form groups. T. Nakamura (volvox)

Holacanthus passer Valenciennes 1846
King angelfish

Holacanthus passer is the representative angelfish from
the East Pacific Ocean. It is distributed more widely than
H. clarionensis and *H. limbaughi*. The number of
individuals has to be huge across such a wide area.
Juveniles of *H. passer* are similar to juveniles of *H.
clarionensis*, but like the adults they have one bold bright
white line on the side, and the body color is darker. By
these two points it is easy to distinguish between both
species. The hybrid cross between *H. passer* and *H.
clarionensis* naturally occurs, but rarely. However a hybrid
between similarly color fishes has almost the same color
as just one of them. Distinguishing the hybrid is not easy.
Mature adults of *Holacanthus passer* are dark black with
metallic blue, and they often form large groups that swim
at the water surface. Juveniles do not join with a group of
adults, hiding around rocks or among corals. Adult males
are longer than females and have white pelvic fins.
Females have yellow pelvic fins. The King angelfish is
very aggressive, and easy to keep in aquariums. The
maximum size is 35.6 cm.

Distribution: Gulf of California, coast of Central America,
Peru, Galapagos Islands, and Ecuador

The size of this juvenile is 3.5cm.

This color morph of *H. passer* is rare. The size is 18cm.

This male has a good body shape and color. The size is 25cm. T. Nakamura (volvox)

Holacanthus limbaughi Baldwin 1963
Clipperton angelfish

Holacanthus limbaughi is observed around Clipperton Island far offshore of Mexico. The body color of adult *H. limbaughi* is dull blue-gray. The most colorful period is juveniles that are essentially a blue variant of *H. passer*. One interesting thing is that the white spot on the body sides does not disappear from juveniles to adults. *Holacanthus passer* has a white line on the same place, and mature males of both species have metallic blue bodies. The body color of adults is almost the same dark gray as juveniles and young adults. The soft dorsal and anal fins have a sharp edge, and the white tails becomes large and develops filaments in mature adults. The trade of *H. limbaughi* is rare, and it is a very expensive fish because the habitat of *H. limbaughi* is very remote. The maximum size is 25 cm.

Distribution: Clipperton Island

The size of this individual is 5cm.

The size of this individual is 30cm.

H. limbaughi makes a nice group in a tank.

Holacanthus africanus Cadenat 1950
Guinean angelfish

The distribution of *Holacanthus africanus* is the Atlantic
Ocean along the coast of West Africa. It is the same
Atlantic Ocean, but the distribution of *H. africanus* does
not overlap the distribution of *H. ciliaris*. *Holacanthus
africanus*, *H. ciliaris*, and *H. bermudenisis* are classified
into the subgenus of *Holacanthus* known as *Angelichthys*.
The adults of *H. africanus* are darker yellowish green like
olives, a unique body color in angelfishes. Juveniles have
an unbelievable body color. The color of juveniles cannot
be imagined from looking at the adults. Juveniles are
shining blue until the size of 4cm. Then the edge of the
body turns to orange, and the blue is lost completely.
After that the body becomes darker yellowish green.
Juveniles and adults have a characteristic "ear-spot" above
the gill operculum. This spot is reminiscent of the same
pattern in *Apolemichthys* spp. The body shape is round
and cute. Then they develop filaments on the soft dorsal
and anal fins like *H. ciliaris*. Large adults have filament
extensions on the tail as well. The size of adults is from 30
to 45cm. *Holacanthus africanus* is seen in the aquarium
trade a few times per year, and is one of the more
expensive angelfishes. It is a very aggressive species, but
also very hardy in captivity.

Distribution: Coast of West Africa from Senegal and Cape
Verde Islands to Congo

The size of this individual is 3.5cm.

The size of this individual is 10cm.

The size of this beautiful adult at Cape Verde Islands is 40cm. T. Nakamura (volvox)

Angelfishes in the Aquarium

This chapter features a selection of beautiful aquariums designed to display angelfishes. It is intended to show a range of possibilities for creating displays that are both functional and beautiful. The aquariums are mainly located in Japan, so the equipment descriptions may not match what is available in other parts of the world, but similar types of equipment appropriately sized can be substituted.

A further intention is to show exhibits that were modeled after nature for keeping extremely rare species. Many of these exhibits are really one-of-a-kind. Having them here in one place offers a tour of tanks that is sure to inspire all enthusiastic angelfish lovers and aquarists.

Tank Data: 600 x 450 x 600(H)mm glass.
Lighting: "Super cool 115" (150W) spot light located at a far distance.
Filtration: Hang on filter, Prism protein skimmer. Power Head (for water flow).
Water temperature: 25°C (adjusting with room air conditioner).
Water exchange: Once a month/approximately 10 liters.

A good tank home for *Centropyge*

When raising an angelfish, it is ideal to be able to get a large tank. However sometimes depending on your budget and space, the ideal condition may not be possible. But if we are considering a long-term commitment and we consider the stress of the fishes, we would like to use a tank that has at least 100 liters in volume. One or two small *Centropyge*, sharing the tank with *Anthias*, a tang, or anemonefish will be good for this kind of tank.

If there are some rocks in the tank, the angelfishes can use that for refuge and swim around areas. If you are able to set up adequate illuminations and filters, it adds interest to include in the layout some corals as well. You will need to create a tank by carefully deciding which types of corals to layout. If you include an overflow and sump, and attach a large protein skimmer, your monthly maintenance will be

Centropyge loricula that naturally inhabits in waters around 20 meters deep does not need strong lighting. It is an easy type to maintain with any artificial foods, and it gets along well with soft corals.

easier. *Centropyge loricula* (subgenus *Xiphypops*) does very little damage to most corals, and is a good fish for beginners. If you have them swim under too strong illumination, their body color becomes blackened.

Tank Data: 1300 x 450 x 500(H)mm acrylic.
Filtration: Over flow, Coral sand filter on the bottom of tank. Main pump RMD45, Power Head (for water flow). UV sterilizing light QL-25.
Water temperature: 24°C (Reisea LX-502CX chiller).
Lighting: Fluorescent light 20W x 1 light.
Water exchange: Once a month/approximately 15 liters.

Genicanthus is a good swimmer

Genicanthus spp. angelfish swim well in the mid-water area of the tank, so you will need a large tank for them to feel comfortable. The best way to set up their tank is to put less rocks and make the water current flow strong. *Genicanthus* males form harems of 4 to 5 females, so if you have a tank with at least 500 liters in volume, you will be able to raise several large females. The wild-caught males tend to be difficult to condition well, so an alternative is to purchase a few females, and then wait patiently for one of them to change sex to a male.

Unlike other angelfishes, *Genicanthus* forage for their food in the middle of the tank, and they need to be fed few times each day. It is good to also have wrasses and scavenger shrimps, or serpent stars at the bottom of the tank, so they

A *Genicanthus bellus* male is rare and difficult to find in the trade. It has a nice sober color.

can clean up by eating any left over food. If you do not put any sand on the bottom, the fishes will find and eat the left over food, so food waste is kept to a minimum.

There is only fluorescent light used on this tank, which is just enough light to view the fishes. Be careful not to provide more light than necessary, because too much will stress them.

Tank Data: 900 x 600 x 00(H)mm glass
Lighting: Coral glow 250W x 2 lights.
Sea swirl 13A (for water flow). Sump: H&S protein skimmer HS850, Knop Calcium reactor C type.
Water temperature: 26°C (Reisea LX-150CX chiller).

Well-balanced mixed environment makes for a colorful aquarium. Let us now develop a tank that has a wide variety of fishes big and small, just like the natural coral reefs. Surely, the main fishes here are the *Pomacanthus asfur* and *Pygoplites diacanthus*, and the other fishes swimming actively around them in a group are *Pseudanthias squamipinnis*. *Pygoplites diacanthus* have a nervous temperament and are relatively difficult to keep. Because of this, we should place them in the tank the earliest, and give them enough time to get used to feeding. Once they are well adjusted to the environment, add the *Pomacanthus asfur*. To help stimulate the appetite of such sensitive fishes, it is a good idea to add smaller fishes with big appetites, such as Damselfish or *Anthias*. These active fishes will cleanly eat up the food left over by the angelfishes, so they are effective in protecting the

Tangs are perfect for cleaning algae in the aquarium. They get along with *Pomacanthus asfur* and *Pygoplites diacanthus* as well.

water quality. Angelfishes generally eat a lot of food in the wild, so it should be even in the tank. You would like to feed them enough till their tummies become round.

By the way, the tank shown is equipped only with a protein skimmer, and it is sustained by the Berlin system. The live rock and sand serve as biological filtration.

Tank Data: 1000 x 600 x 600 (H) mm glass.
Lighting: Coral glow 250W.
Sump: Reef Devil II operating with EHEIM 2215. Main pump is MD-550, MJ-1200 x 2 for water flow).
Water temperature: 25°C (Chiller used).

Raising a *Holacanthus ciliaris* requires careful detail

A tank with various angelfishes gathered from around the world is nice, but it is also a joy to raise your favorite angelfish from juvenile to adulthood. *Holacanthus ciliaris* from Florida are not difficult to raise, but it is a challenge to keep their beautiful body color. In order to maintain their vibrant color, water quality, light, and proper feeding are essential. In general, if it is an environment where the corals can smoothly grow, the *Holacanthus ciliaris* will grow beautifully as well. The most important requirement of all is the water quality, and to be specific, pH over 7.8 and KH over 8. Of course the ammonia and Nitrite Nitrogen must be 0, and a water temperature of 24 to 26°C should be constantly maintained. If these conditions are stabilized, the tank does not have to have corals. Corals can be thought of as a barometer for the water quality. In this tank some Caribbean gorgonians are grown, and they will not be eaten by the *Holacanthus ciliaris*. The main food for this *Holacanthus ciliaris* is a man-made herbivorous fish feed mixed with krill and seaweed.

Holacanthus ciliaris swimming with a tank mate, a young Atlantic tarpon.

After 6 months of growth. Check out the body color and shape.

Tank Data: 900 x 900 x 600(H) mm crystal reef strong glass tank.
Lighting: 150W 10,000K metal halide x 2 lights, RB37 30 x 2 lights, AB 250W 10000K x 1 light, Osram 9W blue x 4 lights.
Sump: E.T.S.S. Evolution 750 protein skimmer, Procal D calcium reactor, IKS Aquastar controller, Dupla float switch, Sea swirl 13A x 2 machines, Pump RMD-551 x 2, RMD-301 (for skimmer).
Water temperature: 25°C (Zensui ZC-1000 chiller).

Can angelfish and coral be raised together?

The tanks we have seen so far have been focused on getting the angelfish`s living environment faithfully realized, and not to just raise angelfishes. Overcrowded tanks should be avoided and raising each individual fish with a lot of attention is the best way for long-term success.

On the other hand, there is a challenge too. This being the interaction between the angelfishes and the corals in the tank. Some angelfishes present no problem with the corals at all, but the larger sized angelfishes will surely injure parts of the corals. Even if the angelfishes poke the corals sometimes, if the condition of the aquarium is good, and the corals are growing normally, it can be said that it is an ideal tank. To help create this condition, you have to feed the angelfishes

Apolemichthys kingi has strong herbivorous preferences.

frequently and in enough quantity, so they don't bother the corals too much, or you can make a tank with mainly live rocks. This photo is of coral and *Apolemichthys* getting along well. It is a good example of adapting the habit of *Apolemichthys kingi*, a herbivore, counting on the idea that it will not poke at SPS corals so much. Nevertheless, their habits change a little, depending on the living conditions. Daily observation is necessary.

Tank Data: 900 x 600 x 580(H) mm acrylic.
Lighting: NZ GP II-04.
Sump: Prism protein skimmer.
Pump: RMD-550 (main), MJ-1200 x 2 (for water flow).
Water Temperature: 24°C (using chiller).

The charm of angelfishes in a dimly illuminated tank
There are coral reefs that have a bright image with sunrays
streaming, and also a dimly lighted zones created by caves
and drop offs. There are many angelfish types that are
adaptable to various environments, and some of them inhabit
caves and deep areas. Aquariums that have these
environmental motifs really look great with corals that do not
need light, such as the non-photosynthetic gorgonians and
Tubastraea spp. At the same time, one should choose
angelfishes that prefer this kind of environment. The angelfish
living in this tank are *Paracentropyge venusta. Centropyge
multicolor* and *C. colini* are also angelfishes that will adapt
well to this tank. Gorgonians and *Tubastraea faulkneri* need
to be fed as well, so it is a good environment for the
angelfishes because they can always get plenty of food and
fill their tummies. Although it is a tank, once the fishes adapt
themselves to the environment they will show their natural

Cirrhilabrus rubrimarginatus and *Paracentropyge venusta*. These are both fishes that prefer dim places.

beauties. Other than *Paracentropyge venusta*, the other fishes
chosen for this tank are wrasse and *Anthias*, because they do
not prefer strong illumination either. The gorgonians are fed
very fine food that will quickly fill up a mechanical filtration
system, so in this tank a Berlin system is used. The skimmer
will cleanse the leftover food, or it will become food for the
cleaner shrimp or lugworm that live on the bottom in the
tank. This aquarium is advantageous because the cost of
illumination electricity is only for the purpose of viewing.

119

Aquarium of Mr. Shimizu in Tokyo, Japan

This small-polyped stony coral dominated aquarium features a deep sandbed, calcium reactor, plenty of light and water motion. The high light intensity necessitates a chiller to maintain the water temperature. It is a perfect habitat for *Centropyge loricula*.

Tank Data: Custom glass aquarium
Lighting: MT-250 x 3, BB450 x 2, RB37 x 1
Water temperature: 24°C (ZC1300 chiller)
Sump: Mini-Cal, RMD400 x 2 (Main Pumps)

A view of the whole display.

Almost all equipment is handmade by the owner.

120

Bartlet Anthias and Flame Angelfish in nice condition.

Caribbean Reef Theme

Although few Caribbean stony corals are available to aquarium hobbyists, the characteristic photosynthetic gorgonians from the region are available, and a wonderful reef scene can be created using them as a focal point. This tall aquarium perfectly shows off a feather-shaped *Pseudopterogorgia*. The hybrid cherub angelfish looks at home here.

Tank Data: Custom glass aquarium 600 x 450 x 600(H) mm
Lighting: MT-150
Water temperature: 25°C
Sump: Berlin Air Lift skimmer, RMD450 (Main Pump)

Aquarium 600 x 450 x 600(H) mm. This tank's concept is "Caribbean Sea".

Maybe this fish is a hybrid of *Centropyge argi* x *C. aurantonota*.

A view of the whole display. It is probably more colorful than this fish's original habitat, but that is not a problem!

Deep Reef Display for *Centropyge narcosis*

Designing a beautiful display for this exceedingly rare deepwater angelfish involves balancing the desire to have a colorful exhibit and the requirement that the light levels be very low, as they are in this fish's natural habitat. Bright light would stress the fish, discourage it from venturing out to feed, and cause its yellow color to become marked with dark spots. Non-photosynthetic gorgonians and stony corals are maintained with planktonic feeds, and some low-light tolerant large-polyped zooxanthellate stony corals are maintained at the border of their natural light requirements. Feeding helps them survive. With adequate food supply and some degree of luck the angelfish will avoid tasting these corals.

Centropyge narcosis don't like brightly illuminated environment.

Lighting: 20W Blue Light
Water temperature: 22°C (LX110GX chiller)
Sump: Wet biological filter system, RMD450 (Main Pump)

A view of the room with this reef aquarium that can be viewed from three sides.

Room-divider aquarium of Mr. Tanda in Osaka, Japan

Very few home aquarists have the opportunity to create a display for a pair of *Chaetodontoplus conspicillatus*. These dream angelfishes great their owner with their sweet faces and lazy swimming manner.

Tank Data: Custom glass aquarium
Lighting: HQI 250W x 1, HQI 150W x 2
Water temperature: 25°C (KDA100T3 chiller)
Sump: MD100RN(Main Pump), Gemini 800, QL40T x 2

Conspicuous Angelfishes are a good pair.

End view of this tank that divides the dining and kitchen area.

The sump is located downstairs.

A pair of *Centropyge joculator* looks at home among the soft corals in this aquarium.

Mushroom Leather Coral Tank

This aquarium featuring a pair of lovely Joculator Angelfish is dominated by a healthy growth of soft corals, *Sarcophyton* spp in particular. The movement of soft coral polyps in the bright light is one of the most attractive natural backgrounds in any marine aquarium. This one is highlighted by the use of natural sunlight too! Of course such a set up requires careful planning to maintain the water temperature.

Tank Data: Custom glass aquarium
Lighting: Natural Sun Light (Tank set outside room)
Temp: 26°C
Sump: Wet Biological Filter System, RMD550 (Main Pump)

Centropyge joculator is beautiful in the bright reef tank.

Cauliflower soft coral needs strong current.

Scribbled Angelfish pair.

Aquarium of Mr. Kamiya in Saitama, Japan

Compared with most reef aquariums, this spectacular display shows a big difference. Instead of having many small corals, this display features old, large coral colonies that nearly fill the space. Likewise, instead of many small fishes, a pair of adult Scribbled angelfish dominates. It is a mature, well-established aquarium that brings joy to anyone who observes it.

Tank data: Acrylic bow-front tank
Lighting: MSO-12502 (HQI 150W x 2, BB450 20W x 4)
Water temperature: 25°C (CL-500 chiller)
Sump: Bicom Buffie Filter, UVF-250, RMD550 (Main Pump)

A view of the filtration and equipment.

Have a seat and watch the show.

The female is below, the male above.

Overview of the display.

Hawaiian Fishes Tank

This aquarium was created to feature Hawaiian fishes, in particular
Hawaiian angelfishes. The corals and zoanthids are of course from
Indonesia, but they are not the main focus of the display. Note the pair
of Hawaiian Flame Angelfishes, which have much more brilliant red
color compared to flame angelfish from other areas. The black and
white Bandit Angelfish makes a beautiful contrast with their red color.

Tank data:

Lighting: HQI 150W, BB450 20W x 2
Water temperature: 25°C (LX-200CX chiller)
Sump: Wet Filter System, RMD450 (Main Pump)

Bandit Angelfish swimming in a soft coral tank.

The sump and filtration equipment are located below the aquarium.

Aquarium of Mr. Nakano in Kyoto, Japan

This small-polyped stony coral dominated reef aquarium features a large fish population, including many angelfishes. This kind of display requires a lot of skill to create and maintain. The corals require careful maintenance of calcium and alkalinity levels and strong lighting and water motion, while the fishes require lots of food, which can pollute the water. With proper filtration controls to prevent accumulation of dissolved inorganic nutrients, the extra food promotes the coral growth.

Tank data: Custom glass aquarium
Lighting: MT-250 x 3, MT150 x 2
Water temperature: 23°C (ZC-700 chiller)
Sump: ETSS Jemini 800+RMD551. KNOP HD calcium reactor, QL-40 x 2, IKS AQUA Controller, RMD201 x 3 (Wave)

The stand is built in with the floor. The lighting system is supported by a rack above the tank.

An adult Clarion Angelfish from Mexico. The size is 22cm.

This community tank houses many healthy and beautiful angelfishes.

138

This healthy Peppermint Angelfish resides in an aquarium created solely for displaying it.

Aquarium of Mr. and Mrs. Uragami in Nagoya, Japan

This small aquarium was created to feature, maintain, and breed the magnificent Peppermint Angelfish, *Centropyge boylei*. Biological filtration is accomplished with live sand and live rock. No corals are grown in this display. The barren rock surfaces resemble the habitat where these fish come from at over 100 meters depth. Because they occur at such depth, where the water is much cooler than at the surface, the water temperature in the tank is maintained with 2 chillers (one serving as a backup in case the other fails).

Peppermint Angelfish have lived for about 7 years in this tank.

Tank data: glass aquarium
Lighting: only Room Light
Water temperature: 22°C (ZC-500 chiller x 2)
Sump: Home made Protein Skimmer

Waikiki Aquarium Coral Farm

This tank is set outside of the Waikiki aquarium on Oahu Island. Inside there are many corals of the genus *Acropora,* and the fishes include *Pomacanthus imperator*, *Holacanthus limbaughi*, *Chaetodon lunula*, and *Zebrasoma flavescens*, among others. It is an enviable tank for all aquarists for its splendid and effective natural system presentation, with stable sunrays and high quality natural ocean water pumped in on a continuous basis.

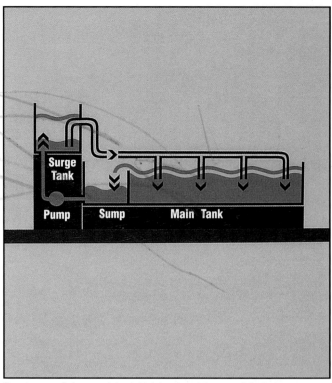

The system uses a Carlson surge device, depicted above, to create long surges in the display.

Angelfish tankmates

Aquariums reveal many expressions. The tank with swimming angelfish completely changes its atmosphere depending on the other tank mates. To make a well-composed tank, you should not randomly choose additional fishes to swim together. Even though the tank is well managed, there are many instances where trouble can develop because a new fish is put in. The first things to be careful about are the introduction of disease such as White Spot, and the compatibility with other fishes already in the tank. The newcomer needs to be put in an isolated area first, and observed for 2 or 3 days. If the fish can settle down and be trained to feed, there is a high probability that the addition in the display aquarium will be successful. Quarantine for a longer period may be needed to reduce the chance of disease outbreak. However, even after that, there are cases of some fishes that get beaten up as soon as they are released in the main tank. Those fishes tend to get sick if you leave them in, and may become a trigger for destroying the whole tank. To prevent such a thing, you should take out the fish as soon as you find out that they do not get along together, or mix in 3 to 4 fishes together all at once, so that the former fishes will not target just one fish. An aquarium is an environment is like a seesaw, and anything can happen. To make such an environment as balanced as possible is the main role of the aquarist who is the keeper.

Stonogobiops dracula and a juvenile of *Pygoplites diacanthus* from the Maldives feed on frozen copepods.

Stream wrasse and *Holacanthus africanus*. They are precious fishes from the Cape Verde Islands in the Atlantic.

Centropyge bispinosa and *Hemiulis rubricephala*. This pretty duo was collected in Sulawesi Indonesia.

Centropyge multicolor and *Cirrhilabrus rhomboidalis*. They both are juveniles and charming.

Larger sized angelfishes dancing in the water. If you are mindful of their power balance, the tank will be very lively.

Juveniles of Blue Potter's Angelfish and *Apolemichthys arcuatus*. Both came from Hawaii.

Centropyge debelius and *Bodianus opercularis*. Both prefer swimming in a low-light environment.

Centropyge colini and *Zebrasoma flavescens*. Angelfish and Tang families together show that they are a cool duo.

A *Labroides dimidiatus* cleaning *Centropyge flavissima*. Cleaner wrasses should be accommodated together depending on the size of the angelfish.

Large angelfish can be mixed with a gentle Nurse shark. *Chaetodontoplus meredithi* is shown here.

Holacanthus ciliaris of St. Paul's Rocks. An experienced aquarist can manage to keep this body color, especially when keeping the fish for the long term.

Keeping and Breeding Angelfishes

In this book, I do not openly say that it is easy to keep angelfishes. However, I think the best way to keep them in an aquarium is to have it mirror their natural environment as closely as possible. If your attitude allows you to imagine that it is easy to just set up a tank in 1 or 2 months, you will not even be successful in keeping small *Centropyge* spp. First of all, before purchasing even one fish, it is important to work on a plan for the aquarium.

While the previous section featured a range of ideas for designing a beautiful display aquarium featuring angelfish, this section details the nitty gritty about keeping them, including filtration methods, buying tips, feeding methods, disease issues, aquarium maintenance requirements, and useful equipment. Some additional special aquariums are featured here as well.

Lastly, breeding angelfishes in captivity is an exciting field that began with a couple of species in the 1970's and continues today, with numerous species. While many hybrids naturally occur in some regions, hybridization in captive breeding offers the potential to develop for aquariums new varieties that would not otherwise occur.

Planning the aquarium

Raising angelfish requires as large a space as possible. You will have to work this out within your budget and the space in your room, but even with small *Centropyge* spp. you will need at least a 100-liter tank to secure enough space for the fish to swim. If you are planning to raise larger-sized fish, you should plan an aquarium that is more than 500 litters in volume. There are acrylic and glass tanks for saltwater fishes, and both have their own characteristics, but neither has a clear advantage for raising angelfishes. Considering the climate in Japan, with seasons when the water evaporates and changes the water density, and water temperatures that are hard to maintain in the wintertime, open top aquariums are difficult to manage.

If you want to mix different types of fishes in your aquarium, first decide the kind of fish you would like, and do not purchase fishes without having a plan. Especially when you want to raise a larger sized angelfish together with others, you will need to think of the power balance between the fishes. Otherwise you may end up destroying the condition of the entire aquarium. Fish that are bullied tend to get sick in a mixed tank. A fish that is not in good condition needs to be taken out for treatment, so the layout in the tank needs to be simple enough to take them out easily. It is difficult to make a relaxing environment for the angelfishes with immoderate tank-mates.

I think of the tank where the angelfishes are living comfortably as one environment. In a tank that is functioning well, natural ecology is functioning even though it may not be visible. For example, bacteria and micro crustacea are breaking down organic substances, and corals are consuming essential components from the water. Angelfish kept in such tanks are beautiful and energetic. In order to raise the angelfish well, do not rush, and first start with careful conditioning of the environment in the tank.

A tank with *Apolemichthys arcuatus* and *Centropyge loricula* swimming. The ratio of the size of the fish and the tank should be approximately as shown.

In a large sized mixed tank, corals can be laid out for decoration, but the water quality needs to be maintained for proper coral husbandry.

A natural system tank with *Pomacanthus navarchus* and *Pygoplites diacanthus* swimming. If you limit the number of living creatures, such tanks can be possible.

By not overcrowding angelfishes in one tank, the tank condition will usually be stable. If you want to keep different kinds of angels, you should set up several tanks. For angelfishes that live in shallow water, layout many corals and make a bright tank for them. For angels that live in deeper ocean environments, it will be good to create a darker and rocky atmosphere. The very best way to keep an angelfish for the long term is to study the habitat of the species, and create an environment in the tank that matches it.

Many angelfishes have the habit of poking the corals and eating their tissues, so it is not advisable to put the angelfishes in a tank with corals as the main theme. When planning to keep angelfish in a coral tank, select types of coral that are difficult for angelfishes to eat. The type of angelfish that can be put in a reef tank is only of the subgenus *Xiphypops* in the genus *Centropyge*. The subgenus *Centropyge* is recommended for a fish-only tank. Swimmer *Genicanthus* do not aggressively poke the corals, and they are a type of fish that is at ease when the illumination is darker, so the best choice for them is to select a coral that prefers the shade. Other middle-sized and large angelfishes need special attention when keeping them with specific corals. In order to have these fishes remain healthy in the same tank with the corals, it is important to first keep the fishes in a separate tank and let them get accustomed to eating man made feed before moving them into the main tank. Even after that, you will need to feed the fishes plenty of food. In a well-conditioned tank, the angelfishes will show you their natural beauty.

A room set up with many tanks. By controlling the temperature in the room, the water temperature in all of the tanks can be adjusted as well. This is a dream space for an aquarist.

A large tank that separates the corals from the angelfishes. The water is shared in the filter below the two tanks. By using this method, you can enjoy both the corals and the fish at the same time.

A Berlin type tank with well grown corals of the genus *Acropora*. Rare pygmy angelfish in the subgenus *Xiphypops, Centropyge joculator* and *Centropyge hotumatua* are raised in this tank.

Selecting the System

Orthodox type

When raising an angelfish, it is best if you have a filter tank of 50 to 80 percent of the tank capacity. Other things that need to be considered are adjusting the amount of filter material, the water transit volume, and creating an environment with stable aerobic bacteria. It is almost impossible to place the plumbing layout of the tank, including the chiller, UV sterilizer, and protein skimmer together with the filter in the space below the aquarium. It is ideal if you can put the main pump and chiller outside and away from the display aquarium. This way the noise, heat, and space will not be a problem. The more complicated the plumbing becomes, the more it needs to be constructed well.

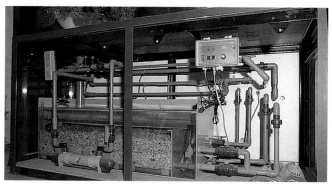

A typical orthodox filter tank. The plumbing is done simply, so that it is easy to maintain. The pump and the chiller are set outside.

There is no special filter system that is best for the angelfishes, but whatever type is used, maintaining the system and managing the water quality is important. You will need to coordinate the filter system based on where to put the tank, what kind of living creatures will be maintained together with the angelfish, how the aquascape is arranged, and what types of corals you are going to have. The choice involves personal preference, understanding of the filter theory, but most important of all is the ease of maintaining the system.

Hybrid type

Another tank that is different from the usual wet/dry filter tank, and used as a natural system sump, sometimes has a little filtration material left when using a protein skimmer. By placing old, live filtration media (gravel or other porous substrates) coated with the aerobic bacteria in a net, it makes for a quick tank start up. Also when starting the Berlin system, if the coral gravel or sand is not well washed, or if you are going to cure a live rock which is starting to spoil, just add a bit of old, live filtration media to help recover the clearness of the water. This filtration material can be taken out when the tank later stabilizes, and then the Berlin system can resume normal function. When starting up the Berlin system, it is not good to have many fishes in the tank. This is even more true when the fishes are not in good condition, because their recovery

A combination of a protein skimmer and a UV sterilizing light on a regular filter sump. By taking out the filtration material, it will be a Berlin system.

will be delayed by poor water quality. In this case, you can put old living biological filtration material with bacteria on it in the filter sump, and it will temporarily protect the water quality. Starting the tank should be performed with much attention and care. If possible, when starting the Berlin system, it is safer to put 1 or 2 test fishes in the tank and observe them.

Berlin type

The Berlin system sump does not use any filtration material at all, and only the large sized protein skimmer is in operation. The bigger the sump, the easier it is to maintain and secure the water quality, but if you try to install everything underneath the tank, there will likely be various problems. Especially, if it is a fully equipped reef tank with a wave function, chiller, and automatic dosing system, the plumbing lay out in the cabinet tends to be complicated. You will need to put identification tapes on the pipes and lines so that it will be easy when you service them.

Angelfishes have comparatively good health when kept in a Berlin system. But, if you have many fishes mixed together, a lot of treatment will be necessary before you

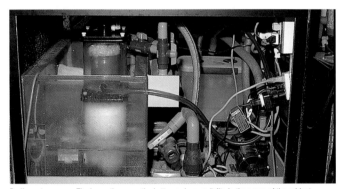

Berlin system sump. The larger the sump the better, as long as it fits in the space of the cabinet.

accommodate all the fishes in the tank. If trouble comes and the White Spot disease breaks out, you should not do any medication inside the Berlin system, but take all the fishes out of the tank and keep on running the Berlin system without any fishes. The White Spot disease will become weak if there is no host fish, so after all the fishes are taken out, it is good to put a cleaner shrimp in the tank to fix the tank's condition. If it is a tank mainly with corals, you should limit the angelfish types to *Centropyge*, so that the ecological balance in the tank will be easier to manage.

Wet type

This style of filtration is called wet type because the filtration material is covered under water. This system can start up a tank quickly because the water can equally flow through the filtration material spread beneath the tank. A wet type system is often used for tanks with many kinds of fishes. When the overflow water passes directly into the filtration material, it can clog it up, so it is better to first let the water go through a mechanical filter such as polyester floss, polyester bag, or reticulated foam sponge. Often coral sands are used for biological filter media, but depending on the power of the pump, adjustment is needed regarding the grain size and the thickness of the sand. If not, beneficial aerobic bacteria will not develop properly to help balance the tank.

It is better for the wet type filter system to have mechanical filtration because it is easier to maintain, and it will be stable for a longer period.

It is also possible to make a multi-layered filter above the tank, and use a dry type filtration material such as bio-balls. But if the wet layer gets clogged, or if you start putting in too many fishes before the bacteria is established, the tank's water condition can rapidly deteriorate. Because of this, the wet layer and the mechanical filter layer needs to be cleaned regularly. To maintain the wet layer, it is best to use something like a gravel vacuum and suck up the detritus in the sand together with the water. You can also be creative and enjoy making a drain board in the bottom of the aquarium to make it easy to clean up.

Useful equipment for angelfish care

Protein skimmer

A protein skimmer is not a device that is used only for natural systems. It is great for any kind of aquarium, and by attaching it to a rapid filter system, it can reduce the burden on the filter. It is effective especially for a tank with fishes that are given a lot of food, because before the fish's waste gets completely dissolved, the protein skimmer will remove most of it. At the same time, the dissolved oxygen level will increase, so it will make the aerobic bacteria active. Depending on the design, it can be added to the original system, so it is an item you would definitely want for angelfish tanks.

A skimmer to hang outside which is a convenient add on, and a larger type that needs plumbing. There are several skimmers with different functions and characteristics. It is better to choose a type with extra capacity than the volume of the tank.

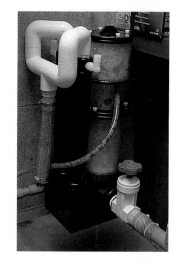

Chiller

An aquarium chiller is one of the most expensive additional pieces of equipment, but using one will give you a lot of security. It is best to get advice from specialty shops, because depending on the manufacturer, they differ in price and cooling capacity. It is ideal to install the chiller outside away from the aquarium because hot air blows out from the machine as it cools the water. If the ventilation is not good, the cooling ability is diminished .

A tank that uses strong illumination such as metal halide lamps often needs to add a chiller, and the percentage of this system combination is growing every year.

Tank chillers are high priority machinery. Many types are available, so you should examine them well before buying.

UV sterilizing lamp

UV sterilizers are very useful for community tanks where many fishes come and go. Even if a new fish brings in a sickness, the ultraviolet rays can control and prevent the spread of it before the other fishes get sick. But if the fish are already sick and need a real treatment, it is not sufficient to depend on the UV sterilizer. In addition, after installing the UV sterilizer the water in the tank becomes clearer. The light bulbs of a UV sterilizer have a certain life span, so it will not be effective if they are not regularly changed. Another important point is to adjust the amount of water that goes through it. A slower flow means a longer contact time and more thorough pathogen kill rate. This must be balanced against the total size of the aquarium. Follow manufacturer recommended guidelines.

The sterilizing power is stronger if the wattage is high, but at the same time, it will also warm up the water. It is important to choose a sterilizing lamp that matches the volume of the tank.

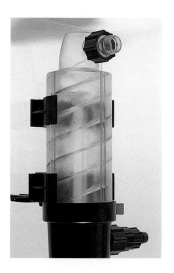

Lighting

The lighting equipment is very important to show the beauty of angelfishes, so the type of illumination selected should depend not only the size of the tank but also the types of fishes. For example, Metal Halide lamps that are beneficial for keeping corals can stress some fishes that inhabit deep water. This type of lamp can also cause the lighter areas of the fishes' body color to turn black, so they need to be installed further away from the tank. Many corals can thrive in an environment with only fluorescent lights. Anyhow, here I would like to demonstrate some suitable lighting options for the angelfishes.

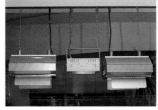

An example using several light systems.

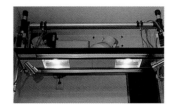

A stylish one bodied type.

Depending on the type of tank, several fluorescent lights may be used.

Calcium reactor

A calcium reactor is not just a device for growing stony corals. This can easily be proven if live rocks are used in the layout. The installation of the reactor will stabilize the KH at a high level. This will activate coralline algae on the surface of the live rocks, and will help maintain good water quality for the angelfishes. To the contrary, if the pH and KH level are low, the body color of the angelfishes will gradually lose its brightness, so together with the ammonia and other common testing parameters, you should also periodically watch the water quality maintained by the reactor, and keep it operating properly.

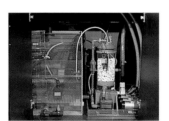

There are different kinds of calcium reactors. It is important to choose one that matches the volume of the tank.

Wave controller

It is beneficial to create a moderate current in the tank. The angelfishes tend to lack exercise in an aquarium, so swimming against a current will improve their appetite, and make them stronger. Generally a power head is used, and controlled with a wave controller. You can adjust and set the current to be a little faster during the day and gentler in the evening. Strong flowing water in the tank is very effective for preventing White Spot disease as well.

Motion current system installed in the water.

Easy to install power heads.

Sea swirl installation for the rim of the tank.

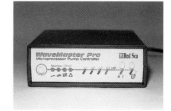

A controller that creates random currents.

Buying Tips

When purchasing an angelfish, you must take your time and select a healthy individual fish. Your long term keeping success depends on this moment of selection. Healthy angelfishes swim quickly, and eagerly look for food on the walls and rocks of the tank. Many angelfishes are imported after going through various processes, so by the time they are in the aquariums in shops they may or may not be in good condition. An excellent shop will make sure to only sell fishes that are conditioned well, and the key to purchasing a good fish is to first find an excellent shop.

There are many varieties of angelfish on sale at the shops, but it is difficult to find an angelfish that matches what you are looking for. You might want to take time to observe its condition, and hope to purchase it in a few days, but often another customer would end up buying it before you. It is ideal if you have a trusting relationship with the shop staff, and have a pipeline to request the angelfish you want.

When accommodating the purchased fish, if you do not have real confidence in its condition, you should not put the fish directly in your display tank. Put the fish into a quarantine or treatment tank, and watch it for 2 to 3 days. Then move it into your fish tank. During that time, carefully check if the fish is eating well and also if it has parasites. After the quarantine period, adjust the water parameters (temperature, salinity, pH) in the quarantine tank matches with the water in the display tank, and then slowly acclimate it. If there is already an angelfish inhabiting the tank, you will need to first put it in a cage and let them meet and see if they get along. This is because before the newcomer gets used to the new tank, the ones that were there before will often abuse it. When it appears that they don't get along well, you will need to try something like getting the former angelfish out of the tank. After that, you can put the newcomer in the tank, and then after 1 or 2 weeks, bring back the former one.

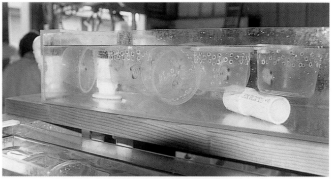
Many angelfishes abroad waiting to be shipped out. The Angels will arrive tired from hours of transportation.

Paracentropyge boylei eating man-made feed. Once the fish is in this condition, the owner can feel relieved.

Angelfishes tend to weaken with mouth injuries, so it is necessary to check both upper and lower jaws. Photo is of *Chaetodontoplus conspicillatus*.

Kinds of food and how to feed

There are various foods you can give to angelfishes. Giving them always the same type will not provide them with a balanced nutrition, so it is best to give them different foods within their range. Until the newly received angelfish starts eating, the new owner is very worried. If it eats krill or the man made feed from the beginning, there is no problem. But a fish that has just arrived usually does not eat aggressively. Especially the large sized *Chaetodontoplus* and *Genicanthus*, and the largest sized *Centropyge* tend to suffer from anorexia after the stress of transportation. If they do not eat immediately after purchasing, these fishes are the ones that aquarists will have great difficulty keeping. There is a tendency that newly purchased angelfish first eat a small amount of feed. It is important to find the foods that they will eagerly eat. Even though the fish itself is large, angelfishes prefer to eat finer delicate feeds. However, no matter how much nutrition the man made feed has, if the food is too hard when the fish bites, it will quickly spit it out.

How the food moves down through the water is an important point too. Usually, angelfish that are not used to being fed hide behind the rocks, so you will need to put the food gently in the current and let it flow. If the feed does not sink at all, or if it sinks too fast, the cautious fish will miss their timing to eat. In that case, it is good if you have other fishes such as Damselfishes, Gobies, or Wrasses that get along with angelfishes, so they can eat the left over feed before it gets spoiled. These fishes have big appetites, and they will jump to eat all kinds of foods. Their enthusiasm helps to release the angelfish's cautiousness, and helps it to start eating. In order to effectively feed the angelfish, it is therefore an important tip to think of the other fishes in the tank.

It is not good if most of the feed just gets trapped in the filter. The left over feed will spoil the water quality rapidly, so if your aquarium has a mechanical filter, you will need to regularly clean it. But if, instead, the feeding is not only for the fishes but also for the worms, shrimps, and crabs in the sand and live rock, there are fewer possibilities for the food to be left over. The environment created will be more natural for the angelfishes. To design the tank as "one environment" is important for the corals as well as the angelfish. In any case, feeding is a joyful time for the owner to be able to recognize the health of the fishes.

Coral feeder, *Centropyge aurantia*.

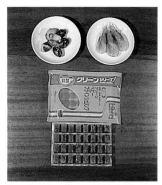

Frozen food, fresh clams and sweet shrimp.

Frozen and minced pink shrimp.

Use krill quickly because it becomes rancid.

Sponges are an angelfish favorite.

Soak only the needed amount of frozen Copepods.

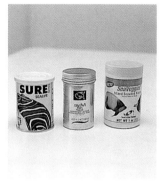

It is wise to use various kinds of feeds.

Sickness and daily maintenance

Here are some of the reasons why angelfish get sick and die in aquariums: A disease outbreak after a newly introduced fish. Unstable water temperature due to seasonal changes. The corals and live rocks fouled. Addition of new, uncured pieces. A dead fish was left in the tank and fouled the water quality. A bad injury to the angelfish when it was collected and handled. Physical damage caused by another fish etc. Poor nutrition.

When sickness occurs, you will need to take the fish out of its tank and have it treated. The most common sickness of fishes is the White Spot disease (*Cryptocaryon*). This sickness is caused by cilate parasites. When the white spots on the fishes are visible, the disease is already in its middle stage. In the early stages of White Spot disease, these symptoms will show: Respiration becomes faster, and the fishes rub their bodies to the rocks The pectoral fins become white and dull. The fishes will start swimming with their fins folded, or they will swim against the current lethargically. When you see these early stage symptoms, quickly take the fish out, and give it a medicinal bath with Nitrofurazone and Sulfamerazine sodium according to stated dosages on supplier packaging. If the tank is in good condition, a very slight case of White Spot disease will naturally cure, so use your judgment to decide if an early stage treatment is necessary. If the condition is mild, it is possible to build the fishes' resistance by feeding them more frequently, so long as the water quality is not harmed. Nutrition is an important factor in disease prevention. Also, certain fishes, for example surgeonfishes (*Acanthurus* spp.) that are very prone to White Spot disease should be removed from the aquarium in case of an outbreak, and not returned to the aquarium until after the outbreak has been cured for at least a couple of months. The use of a diatomaceous earth filter can effectively remove the free swimming parasites in small aquariums (less than 100 gallons.

Use copper sulfate for treating angelfishes as the very last resort. It is a very strong treatment that you should avoid if possible. Misuse can hasten the fish's death, and even if the sickness gets cured, there is a chance of side effects such as development of pits on the body (lateral line erosion), or the color of the body can be ruined. For angelfish health it is indispensable to judge and apply an early stage treatment, as well as to prevent the occurrence of sickness.

Centropyge loricula is with an early stage of White Spot disease. In this tank, it was naturally cured without any medication.

Incompatible mixing of fishes can easily lead to an outbreak of sickness. You should always check the living situation of the fish.

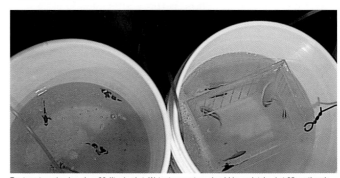
Treatment can be done in a 20-liter bucket. Water temperature should be maintained at 25 centigrade, and once every 10 to 15 hours, there is need to change the entire water.

Holacanthus ciliaris with Popeye. Natural cures are possible by improving the water quality.

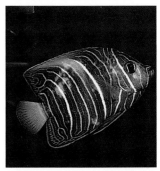
Juvenile of *Pomacanthus* spp. tend to get a keloid like bruises on their bodies.

There are several diseases that affect angelfishes, but if you are able to conquer White Spot disease then there is a high possibility of having a successful tank. In order to prevent White Spot disease the most important thing is to stabilize the water temperature. This is not easy to do, especially in early summer and autumn time when the temperature difference from day to night is wide. It is difficult to maintain the water temperature without a chiller for the tank. However, a well kept fish does not get White Spot disease even though there may be a 2 °C fluctuation in water temperature. This is because by getting used to the environment and becoming well acclimated, the mucous secretion on the body surface becomes stabilized, and the fish is more resistant to viruses and other pathogenic organisms. Fishes that are in good condition when purchased have a normal mucous membrane on their bodies.

In order to relax the angelfishes, it is effective to put shrimps and fishes that clean the angelfishes in the tank. These creatures cleanse the angelfish's body surface, gills, and inside the mouth daily, and this exterminates the parasites. Some of these helpful creatures also eat the leftover food from the bottom of the tank both day and night, so they are useful to prevent the water from getting spoiled. However, cleaner wrasse species such as *Labroides dimidiatus* are a little bit persistent, and can be disliked by healthy angelfishes. Observe the situation and take them out if they aren't needed.

Even if the angelfishes are well maintained, the seawater composition changes with time in the aquarium, so it is important to regularly add some components and perform water changes. Iodine (in the form of potassium iodide) helps maintain the fish's body color, and additives that promote high pH and KH levels are very effective not only for the corals but for the angelfishes. I do not want to recommend carelessly, but including some live corals in the tank is a good barometer for keeping an eye on the water quality. Additionally, in a tank that can maintain good water quality, even without corals, purple coralline algae will grow on the rocks, so the layout will look natural as well. If you can manage the water quality in the tank, you will be able to raise the angelfishes more beautifully.

A *Labroides dimidiatus* that is cleaning the gills *of Pomacanthus sexstriatus*.

Small glass shrimp clean the angelfishes well too

A cleaner shrimp cleaning an Arabian Angel. The shrimps clean the fishes with a soft touch, so they do not mind.

It is important to use additives sold in stores to effectively maintain the water quality.

Breeding of *Centropyge* spp.
Photos by Frank Baensch (Reef Culture Technologies LLS)

Frank Baensch is a marine biologist who has researched the propagation of angelfishes for a long time. He has succeeded in continuous breeding of *Centropyge* spp. The commercial propagation of clownfish is easier by comparison because they live in a small space, lay eggs on a substrate, and the larvae are large. Angelfishes spawn in the water column. A pair needs enough space for spawning. The depth has to be over 50cm for the breeding tank because a pair swims upward quickly during the climax. The pair spawns before every sunset during a breeding season. The key point is making an artificial dusk condition. The fertilized egg floats because it is filled with oil, so the tank can be designed to collect the eggs easily. The fertilized eggs go to the filter in the normal tank without any special equipment. Baensch made aquariums out of plastic barrels. The fertilized eggs pass to a collecting tank via the over flow drain. The next morning the collected fertilized eggs are moved to a beaker with rinsing fresh salt water. During this period, good eggs float and come together to the brim of the beaker. These good eggs are then moved to the larval rearing tank. The fertilized eggs float because this keeps them in the zone where the food is available to the larvae. The small planktonic food organisms they eat come to the surface. The larvae hatch in the first day, but don't feed until the eyes develop a few days later. Up to that time they depend on the oil for nutrition. The larvae grow and change form many times. The larvae stay near the surface until they reach a critical stage. They require approximately 60 days after hatching to become juveniles that resemble an adult fish. The larvae of *Centropyge* spp. are smaller than many other marine fish larvae, and raising them takes time and effort. Keeping always a lot of small plankton in the water column is important, as is maintaining water quality. In addition, feeding the spawning parents a nutritious diverse seafood diet including fish eggs, *Spirulina*, and astaxanthin increases the rate of hatch. Before metamorphosis the larvae eat only live plankton, so the equipment to culture plankton is set in the breeding room.

Using these techniques Frank has spawned and reared *C. fisheri, C. loricula, C. resplendens, C. interrupta, C. debelius, C. colini, C. multicolor*, and a hybrid cross of *C. resplendens* and *C. fisheri*. He has also reared the larvae of *Paracentropyge multifasciata* and *Apolemichthys arcuatus*.

Frank Baensch's breeding room, more than 40 tanks.

The egg collector has a net at the bottom.

An original 209 L barrel tank for breeding has an over flow system. The water with the fertilized eggs goes to the collecting egg tank, and then the water goes to the plenum filter.

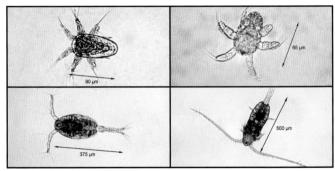
Cultured plankton. The size of the plankton used is changed depending on the size of juveniles.
Photos: Frank Baensch (Reef Culture Technologies LLS)

This breeding pair of *C. interrupta* came from Wakayama, Japan.

Cultured juveniles of *C. interrupta* 80 days after hatching.

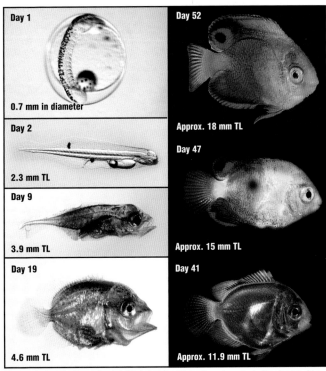

Day 1

0.7 mm in diameter

Day 2

2.3 mm TL

Day 9

3.9 mm TL

Day 19

4.6 mm TL

Day 52

Approx. 18 mm TL

Day 47

Approx. 15 mm TL

Day 41

Approx. 11.9 mm TL

Metamorphosis of *C. interrupta* from hatching to fry, taking 52 days for metamorphosis. The oil phase of the egg is a nutrient for early fry.

C. multicolor pair from the Marshall Islands.

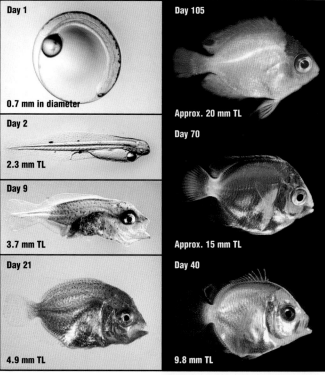

Day 1 0.7 mm in diameter	**Day 105** Approx. 20 mm TL
Day 2 2.3 mm TL	**Day 70**
Day 9 3.7 mm TL	Approx. 15 mm TL
Day 21 4.9 mm TL	**Day 40** 9.8 mm TL

Fry of *C. multicolor*. Before metamorphosis the body turns gold.

Juvenile of *C. multicolor* looks like a miniature adult.

The pair that produced the hybrid cross of *C. resplendens* and *C. fisheri*. J. Coppolino

Hybrid of *C. resplendens* and *C. fisheri*. A. Honn

Larval stages for *Pomacanthus arcuatus* from egg to settlement. M. A. Moe Jr.

Juveniles of the hybrid cross between *Pomacanthus paru* and *P. arcuatus*. M. A. Moe Jr.

Breeding of *Pomacanthus* spp.

For the breeding of large angelfishes such as *Pomacanthus* and *Holacanthus*, a large tank is needed. However these large angelfishes have the same spawning method as the *Centropyge* spp., so the possibility of breeding them is high with good equipment, sufficient space, and parents maintained in good condition. In the mid 1970's Martin A. Moe Jr. obtained eggs and sperm from wild-caught adults of the Gray Angelfish, *Pomacanthus arcuatus* and reared many juveniles. He and Forrest Young also produced hybrids of the French and Gray Angelfish. They could not find gravid females of *Pomacanthus paru* on the reefs in the Florida Keys, but they could find fertile males, and they mixed the *P. paru* sperm with the eggs from *P. arcuatus*. The gametes were carefully pressed from the abdomen of the fish into a container, then the fertilized eggs were rinsed and placed in a rearing tank.

Pomacanthus maculosus and *Chaetodontoplus septentrionalis* have been reared in captivity in Taiwan, in large saltwater ponds with large quantities of plankton. Not much more is known about the techniques used.

Oddly patterned subadult of the hybrid cross between *Pomacanthus paru* and *P. arcuatus*. M. Moe Jr.

A subadult tank-raised white-banded morph of *P. maculosus* from Taiwan.

I am not an ichthyologist or researcher, but I am an aquarist. Who are we aquarists? We like fishes very much. If the coral reef were in front of our home, we would go diving to meet with them everyday, and would not need to have an aquarium at home. Aquarists often dream of that kind of life. If they have enough money and time, they may frequently go diving somewhere to have this experience. The reality is that aquarists are busy every day, and do not often have time for such travel. Therefore they want to spend time each day with fishes by having their own tank at home. A tank and equipment for an aquarium are not cheap, but think about the total cost of several trips, and the cost of an aquarium is not so expensive.

Recently many eager fish watchers have developed. Divers and guides report much information, and some information is precious. The Internet is getting popular, and photographs of rare fishes are showing up on various websites. Some photographs in *Marine Aquarist* that I am editing are provided by divers. The divers supply photographs of rare fishes that are not traded for aquariums. Especially the underwater photographer Tsuneo Nakamura has spent a great deal of time travelling to meet with angelfishes, twice with me. Some precious photographs were taken in these travels, and these photographs make this book much better. Brazilian aquarist Stephen Altit introduced me to Osmar Junior who knew St. Paul's Rocks. Frank Baensch in Hawaii provided information of breeding the genus *Centropyge*. I want to say thank you to all of them. I should not forget traders and shops who support the aquarium hobby with passion, and the many home aquarists. Most of the photographs in this book are taken in aquariums, not in nature. The fishes are very lively in aquariums, the same as in nature. This is one of the charms of aquariums. I hope that the improvement of our aquarium hobby continues to make contributions to research and discoveries in ichthyology.

Kiyoshi Endoh
October, 2003

Kiyoshi Endoh, March 2007

Aburto-Oropeza, O., Sala, E., and C. Sanchez-Ortiz. 2000. Feeding behavior, habitat use, and abundance of the angelfish *Holacanthus passer* (Pomacanthidae) in the southern Sea of Cortez. *Env. Biol. Fish.* 57:435-442.

Aldenhoven, J.M. 1986. Different reproductive strategies in a sex-changing coral reef fish *Centropyge bicolor* (Pomacanthidae). *Aust. J. Mar. Freshwat. Res.* 37:353-360.

Allen, G.R. 1980. *Butterfly and Angelfishes of the World.* Vol 2. Atlantic Ocean, Caribbean Sea, Red Sea and the Indo-Pacific. John Wiley & Sons, New York. 352 pp.

Allen, G.R. and D.R. Robertson. 1994. Fishes of the Tropical Eastern Pacific. Univ. Hawaii Press, Honolulu, 332 pp.

Allen, G.R., Steene, R., and M. Allen. 1998. *A Guide to Angelfishes Åï Butterflyfishes. Odyssey Publishing.*

Allen, G.R., Steene, R., Humann, P., and N. Deloach. 2003. *Reef Fish Identification: Tropical Pacific.* New World Publ./Odyssey Publ. 457 pp.

Allen, G. R., F. Young & P. L. Colin. 2006. *Centropyge abei*, a new species of deep-dwelling angelfish (Pomacanthidae) from Sulawesi, Indonesia. *Aqua, J. Ichthy. Aquat. Biol.* v. 11 (no. 1): 13-18.

Arai, H. 1994. Spawning behavior and early ontogeny of a pomacanthid fish, *Chaetodontoplus duboulayi*, in an aquarium. *Japan J. Ichthyol.* 41:181-187.

Arelland-Martinez, M., Ceballos-Vazquez, B.P., Garcia-Dominguez, F., and F. Galvan-Magana. 1999. Reproductive biology of the King Angelfish *Holacanthus passer* Valenciennes 1846 in the Gulf of California, Mexico. *Bull. Mar. Sci.* 65: 677-685.

Baensch, F. 2002. The Culture and Larval Development of Three Pygmy Angelfish Species. *Freshwater and Marine Aquarium Magazine.* Vol. 25. No. 12: pp 4 – 12 .

Baensch, F. 2003. Marine Copepods and the Culture of Two New Pygmy Angelfish Species. *Freshwater and Marine Aquarium Magazine.* Vol. 26. No. 7: pp 156 – 162.

Bauer, J.A. Jr. and S.E. Bauer. 1981. Reproductive biology of pigmy angelfishes of the genus Centropyge (Pomacanthidae). *Bull. Mar. Sci.* 31: 495-513.

Bellwood, D.R., van Herwerden, L., and N. Konow. 2004. Evolution and biogeography of marine angelfishes (Pisces: Pomacanthidae). *Molecular Phylogenetics and Evolution* 33 (2004) 140–155.

Bellwood, D.R., 1996. The Eocene fishes of Monte Bolca: The earliest coral reef fish assemblage. *Coral Reefs* 15, 11–19.

Bertschy, A. 1997. Notes on the adult coloration in the Annularis Angelfish (*Pomacanthus annularis*). *Sea Scope* 14 (Winter):1, 4.

Blasiola, G.C. Jr. 1976. *Centropyge aurantonotus*, Burgess, 1974 (Pisces: Chaetodontidae) range extension and redescription. *Bull. Mar. Sci.* 26:564-568.

Brockman, H.J. and J.P. Hailman. 1976. Fish cleaning symbiosis: notes on the juvenile angelfishes (Pomacanthus, Chaetodontidae) and comparisons with other species. *Z. Tierpsychol.* 42:129-138.

Burgess, W.E. 1974. Evidence for the elevation to family status of the angelfishes (Pomacanthidae), previously considered to be a subfamily of the butterflyfish family, Chaetodontidae. *Pac. Sci.* 28(1): 57-71.

Burgess, W. E., 1991. Two New Genera of Angelfishes, Family Pomacanthidae. *Tropical Fish Hobbyist.* March 1991:68-70

Campbell, D. 1978. *Pomacanthus annularis. Freshwater and Marine Aquarium.* 1 (8):11-12.

Campbell, D. 1981. Marines: their care and keeping—*Holacanthus-Apolemichthys*: Part 1. *Freshwater and Marine Aquarium* 4(3):22-25.

Campbell, D. 1981. Marines: their care and keeping—*Pomacanthus. Freshwater and Marine Aquarium* 4(9):30-34.

Carlson, B.A. and L.R. Taylor, Jr. 1981. Holacanthus griffisi, a new species of angelfish from the central Pacific Ocean. *Freshwater and Marine Aquarium* 4(10):8-11.

Chung, K.C., Woo, N.Y.S., 1998. Phylogenetic relationships of the Pomacanthidae (Pisces: Teleostei) inferred from allozyme variation. J. Zool. 246, 215–231.

Conde, B. 1986. Longevity of marine tropicals at the Nancy Aquarium. *Sea Scope* 3 (Summer): 1-3.

Conde, B. 1990. Elevage et evolution d'un Hybride presume entre *Pomacanthus maculosus* et *P. semicirculatus. Rev. fr. Aquariol.* 16:117-122.

Conde, B. 1993. A double sex inversion in *Genicanthus lamarck* (Pomacanthidae). Sea Scope 10 (Spring):3.

Debelius, H. 1997. *Mediterranean and Atlantic Fish Guide*, Ikan.

Debelius, H., Tanaka, H., and R.H. Kuiter. 2003. *Angelfishes: A Comprehensive Guide to the Pomacanthidae*. TMC Publishing, Chorleywood, UK, 208 pp.

DeLoach, N. 1999. *Reef Fish Behavior*. New World Publishing, Inc. Jacksonville, Fl, USA. 359 pp.

Dennis, G.D. and T.J. Bright. 1988. Reef fish assemblages on hard banks in the northeastern Gulf of Mexico. *Bull. Mar. Sci.* 43:280-307.

Ehrlich, P.R., Talbot, F.H., Russell, B.C. & G.R.V. Anderson. 1977. The behaviour of chaetodontid fishes with special reference to Lorenz's "poster colouration" hypothesis. *J. zool., Lond.* 183:213-228.

Emmens, C.W. 1972. Pacific angelfish. *Marine Aquarist* 3(1):72.

Emmens, C.W. 1983. Large Pacific angelfishes. *TFH* 3/83.

Feddern, H.A. 1968. Hybridization between the Western Atlantic angelfishes, *Holacanthus isabelita* and *H. ciliaris. Bull. Mar. Sci.* 18(2):351-382.

Fenner, R. M. 1998. *The Conscientious Marine Aquarist*. Microcosm, VT. 432pp.

Fraser-Brunner, A. 1933. A revision of the chaetodont fishes of the subfamily Pomacanthinae. *Proc. Zool. Soc. Lond.* 1933:543-599.

Fricke, H.W. 1980. Juvenile-adult colour patterns and coexistence in the territorial coral reef fish *Pomacanthus imperator. P.S.Z.N.I.:Mar.Ecol.* 1:133-141.

Gronell, A.M. and Colin, P.L. 1985. A toroidal vortex for gamete dispersion in a marine fish, *Pygoplites diacanthus* (Pisces: Pomacanthidae). Anim. Behav. 33:1021-1023.

Hemdal, J. 1989. Marine angelfish: color and style. *Aquarium Fish Magazine*. 1(8):15-20.

Hioki, S. 1992. *Studies on the reproductive behavior and hermaphroditism of Japanese angelfishes*. Ph.D. Dissertation, Kyushu Univ., Fukuoka, 244 pp.

Hioki, S. & K. Suzuki. 1995. Spawning behavior, eggs, larvae, and hermaphroditism in the angelfish, *Apolemichthys trimaculatus*, in captivity. *Bull. Inst. Oceanic Res. & Dev.*, Tokai Univ. 16:13-22.

Hioki, S., Suzuki, K., & Y. Tanaka. 1990. Development of eggs and larvae in the angelfish, *Centropyge ferrugatus. Japan J. Ichthyol.* 37(1):34-38.

Hirata, T., Yamakawa, T., Iwata, A., Manabe, S., Hirmatsu, W., and N. Ohnishi. 1996. Fish fauna of Kashiwa-jima Island, Kochi Prefecture, Japan. *Bull. Mar. Sci. and Fish*. Kochi Univ. 16:177pp.

Hourigan, T.F. and C.D. Kelly. 1985. Histology of the gonads and observations on the social behavior of the Caribbean angelfish *Holacanthus tricolor. Mar. Biol.* 88:311-322.

Howe, J.C. 1993. A comparative analysis of the feeding apparatus in pomacanthids, with special emphasis of oesophageal papillae in *Genicanthus personatus. J. Fish Biol.* 43:593-602.

Humann, P. and N. DeLoach. 2002. *Reef Fish Identification* (Third Edition). New World Publishing, Inc. Jacksonville, FL, USA. 481 pp.

Karanikas, J. 1989. The spawning of the Flame Angelfish *Centropyge loriculus. Sea Scope*, 7:1-2.

Kerstich, A. 1977. Butterflies and angels of the Sea of Cortez. *Marine Aquarist*. 7:17-28.

King, D. 1997. *Reef Fishes & Corals*. Struik Publishers. P/L. Cape Town.

King, D. 2002. *More Reef Fishes & Nudibranchs*. Struik Publishers. P/L. Cape Town.

Kishimoto, H. Hioki, S. & K. Suzuki. 1996. Transfer of *Centropyge multispinis* (Teleostei, Pomacanthidae) from subgenus *Xiphypops* to subgenus *Centropyge. Ichthyol. Res.* 43(2):153-159.

Kosaki, R.K. & D. Toyama. 1987. Gold morphs in *Centropyge* angelfish. *Freshwater Mar. Aquar.* 10(7): 8-11.

Kosaki, R.K. 1989. *Centropyge nahackyi*, a new species of angelfish from Johnston Island (Teleostei: Pomacanthidae). *Copeia*, 1989:880-886.

Krupp, F. and H. Debelius. 1990. The hybrid of *Centropyge multifasciatus* x *Holacanthus venustus* from the Philippines and notes on aberrant colour forms of *Centropyge multispinis* from the Maldives and the Red Sea. *Revue Fr. Aquariol.* 17(2): 53-56.
Kubota, O. 1998. Holacanthus clarionensis. Salt & Sea 25 (Winter): 10-16. (In Japanese)

Kuiter, R.H. 1990. A new species of angelfish (Pomacanthidae) *Chaetodontoplus meredithi*, from eastern Australia. *Revue fr. Aquariol.* 16:113-116.

Kuiter, R.H. 1992. *Tropical reef-fishes of the western Pacific Indonesia and adjacent waters.* Penerbit PT Gramedia Pustaka Utama, Jakarta.

Kuiter, R.H. 1996. *Guide to sea fishes of Australia.* New Holland Publishers, Australia.

Kuiter, R.H. 1998. *Photo Guide to Fishes of the Maldives.* Atoll Editions. Apollo Bay.

Kuiter, R.H. 1998b. A new pygmy angelfish (Teleostei: Perciformes: Pomacanthidae) from the Coral Sea. *Aqua.* 3:85-88.

Kuiter, R.H. 2000. *Coastal Fishes of Southeastern Australia.* Gary Allen ty Ltd. Sydney, Australia.

Kuiter, R.H. and H. Debelius. 1994. *Southeast Asia Tropical Fish Guide.* IKAN-Unterwasserarchiv, Germany.

Lamm, D.R. 1984. Spawning of the Coral Beauty Angelfish. *Sea Scope* 1 (Summer):1-3

Lieske, E. and R.F. Myers. 1994. Collins Pocket Guide. *Coral Reef Fishes: Indo-Pacific and Caribbean.* Harper Collins Publishers, London, 400pp.

Lobel, P.S. 1978. Diel, lunar, and seasonal periodicity in the reproductive behavior of the pomacanthid fish, *Centropyge potteri*, and some other reef fishes in Hawaii. *Pac. Sci.* 32(2):193-207.

Lutnesky, M. 1989. Stimulation, inhibition, and induction of early sex change in the pomacanthid angelfish, *Centropyge potteri*. *Abst.* Albert Tester Paper Series. *Pac. Sci.* 43:196-197.

Lutnesky, M. 1991. A temporal-polygny-threshold model and spawning in the pomacanthid angelfish, Centropyge potteri. *Abst.* Albert Tester Paper Series. *Pac. Sci.* 45:97-98.

Martinez-Diaz, S.F. and H. Perez-Espana. 1999. Feasible mechanism for algal digestion in the King Angelfish. *J. Fish. Biol.* 55:692-703.

Masuda, H., ed. 1987. *The Fishes of the Japanese archipelago.* Oxford Univ. Press. 842. Pp.

McKenna, S. 1990. Keeping the Flamboyant French Angel. *TFH* 1/90.

Michael, S.W. 2004. *Angelfishes & Butterflyfishes.* Reef Fishes Series. T.F.H. Publications, Neptune City, NJ. 344 pp.

Miklosz, J. C. 1972. When is a Koran, not a Koran? *Marine Aquarist* 3(4):72.

Miller, G. 1985. Angelfish of the Caribbean. *Freshwater and Marine Aquarium* 8/85

Moe, M.A. Jr. 1982. *The Marine Aquarium Handbook: Beginner to Breeder.* Green Turtle Publications. 170pp.

Moe, M.A. Jr. 2003. The Breeders Net. A New Dawn for the Culture of Marine Ornamental Fish. http://www.advancedaquarist.com/issues/july2003/breeder2.htm accessed June 2007.

Moe, M. A., Jr. 1976. Rearing Atlantic Angelfish *Marine Aquarist* 7:7, 1976

Moenich, D. R. 1987. Angel food; the most important single factor in keeping marine angels healthy is a varied diet. *TFH* 6/87.

Moenich, D. R. 1988. Breaking the rules (on mixing angel species). *TFH* 3/88.

Moyer, J.T. 1981. Interspecific spawning of the Pygmy Angelfishes *Centropyge shepardi* and *Centropyge bispinosus* at Guam. *Micronesica* 17(1-2):119-124.

Moyer, J.T. 1984. Reproductive behavior and social organization of the pomacanthid fish *Genicanthus lamarck* at Mactan Island, Philippines. *Copeia,* 1984:194-200.

Moyer, J.T. 1990. Social and reproductive behavior of *Chaetodontoplus mesoleucus* (Pomacanthidae) at Bantayan Island, Philippines. *Japan J. ichthyol.* 36:459-467.

Moyer, J.T. & A. Nakazono. 1978. Population structure, reproductive behavior, and protogynous hermaphroditism in the angelfish *Centropyge interruptus* at Miyake-jima, Japan. *Japan J. Ichthyol.* 25(1): 25-39.

Moyer, J.T., Thresher, R.E., and P.L. Colin. 1983. Courtship, spawning and inferred social organization of American angelfishes (genera *Pomacanthus, Holacanthus* and *Centropyge*; Pomacanthidae). *Env. Biol. Fish.* 9:25-39.

Munday, P.L., Jones, G.P., 1998. The ecological implications of small body size among coral reef fishes. Oceanogr. *Mar. Biol. Annu. Rev.* 36, 373–411.

Myers, R.F. 1999. *Micronesian Reef Fishes*: A comprehensive Guide to the Coral Reef Fishes of Micronesia, 3rd revised and expanded edition. Coral Graphics, Barrigada, Guam. 330 pp.

Nakabo, Tetsuji, 2002. *Fishes of Japan with Pictorial keys to the species*, English edition. Tokai Univ. Press. Tokyo.

Neudecker, S. & P.S. Lobel. 1982. Mating systems of chaetodontid and pomacanthid fishes at St. Croix. *Z. Tierpsychol.* 59: 299-318.

Ogilby, J.D. 1915. Review of the Queensland Pomacanthinae. *Mem. Qld. Mus.* 3: 99-116.

Okamura, H. and K Amaoka. 1997. *Yama-Kei Colored Atlas: Marine Fish in Japan*. Yama-Kei Publishers.

Parker P (1994) The rediscovery of the Ballina Angelfish *Chaetodontoplus ballinae*, two new fish records for Lord Howe Island, Australia. *Freshwater and Marine Aquarium* August: 112-115.

Pérez-España, H.A., and L.A. Abitia-Cardenas. 1996. Description of the digestive tract and feeding habits of the King Angelfish and the Cortez Angelfish. *J. Fish. Biol.* 48:807-817.

Pyle, R.L. 1989. Rare and Unusual Marines: Griffis' Angelfish, *Apolemichthys griffisi* (Carlson and Taylor). *Freshwater and Marine Aquarium* 12(3):96-98.

Pyle, R.L. 1989b. Rare and Unusual Marines: The Armitage Angelfish, *Apolemichthys armitagei* —Smith. *Freshwater and Marine Aquarium* 12(4):26-27.

Pyle, R.L. 1989c. Rare and Unusual Marines: The Goldflake Angelfish, *Apolemichthys xanthopunctatus* —Burgess. *Freshwater and Marine Aquarium* 12(5):26-27.

Pyle, R.L. 1990. Rare and Unusual Marines: The Japanese Pygmy Angelfish, *Centropyge interruptus* (Tanaka). *Freshwater and Marine Aquarium* 13(3):32-37.

Pyle, R.L. 1990b. Rare and Unusual Marines: The Masked Angelfish, *Genicanthus personatus* Randall. *Freshwater and Marine Aquarium* 13(10):112-118.

Pyle, R.L. 1992. Rare and unusual marines: a hybrid angelfish *Centropyge flavissimus* x *eibli. Freshwater Mar. Aquar.* 15(3):98-110,212.

Pyle, R.L. 1992b. The Peppermint Angelfish, *Centropyge boylei* n.sp. Pyle and Randall. *Freshwater and Marine Aquarium* 15(7):16-18.

Pyle, R.L. 1992c. Rare and unusual marines: another hybrid angelfish *Centropyge loriculus* x *potteri. Freshwater Mar. Aquar.* 15(8): 40-45.

Pyle, R.L. 1994. Rare and Unusual Marines: The Narc Angelfish, *Centropyge narcosis* n.sp. Pyle and Randall. *Freshwater and Marine Aquarium* 17(4):8-19.

Pyle, R.L. and J.E. Randall, 1993. A new species of *Centropyge* from the Cook Islands, with a redescription of *Centropyge boylei. Revue fr. Aquariol.* 19(4):115-124.

Pyle, R.L. & J.E. Randall. 1994. A review of hybridization in marine angelfishes (Perciformes: Pomacanthidae). *Env. Biol. of Fishes.* 41:127-145.

Randall, J.E. 1975. A revision of the Indo-Pacific angelfish genus *Genicanthus*, with descriptions of three new species. *Bull. Mar. Sci.* 25(3):393-421.

Randall, J.E. and W.D. Hartman. 1968. Sponge-feeding fishes of the west Indies. *Mar. Biol.* 1, 216-225.

Randall, J.E. & F. Yasuda. 1979. *Centropyge shepardi*, a new angelfish from the Mariana and Ogasawara Islands. *Japan. J. Ichthyol.* 26: 55-61.

Randall, J.E., Allen, G.R., and R.C. Steene. 1997. *Fishes of the Great Barrier Reef and Coral Sea*. University of Haewaii Press, Honolulu, 557 pp.

Randall, J.E., Ida, H., Kato, K., Pyle, R.L.,º and J.L. Earle, 1997 Annotated checklist of inshore fishes of the Ogasawara Islands. *Nat. Sci. Mus. Monogr.* (11):1-74.

Reese, E.S. 1973. Duration of residence by coral reef fishes on "home" reefs. *Copeia* (1): 145-149.

Reynolds, W.W. 1979. Habitat selection and territorial defense behaviors in juvenile Cortez Angelfish, *Pomacanthus zonipectus. Hydrobiol.* 66:145-148.

Reynolds, W.W. and L.J. Reynolds. 1977. Observations on the food habits of the angelfishes, *Pomacanthus zonipectus* and *Holacanthus passer* in the Gulf of California. *Calif. Fish and Game*, 63:124-125.

Russell, B.C., Allen, G.R., & H.R. Lubbock. 1976. New cases of mimicry in marine fishes. *J. Zool., Lond.* 180:407-423.

Sala, E., O. Aburto-Oropeza O., and J.L. Arreola-Robles. 1999. Observations of a probable hybrid angelfish of the genus *Holacanthus* from the Sea of Cortez, Mexico. *Pac. Sci.* 53:181-184.

Sano, M., Shimizu, M., and Y. Nose. 1984. Food habits of teleostean reef fishes on Okinawa Island, southern Japan. *Univ. Mus. Univ.* Tokyo Bull. 15, 70 pp.

Sazima, I., Moura-Rodrigo, L., and C. Sazima. 1999. Cleaning activity of juvenile angelfish, *Pomacanthus paru*, on the reefs of the Abrolhos Archipelago, Western South Atlantic. *Env. Biol. Fish.* 56:399-407.

Schaefer, F. 1998. A new Atlantic angel. Aqualog News 18 (April):1-2.

Schiller, G. 1989. Sexual changes in the Angelfish *Genicanthus bellus. Atoll* (*J. Mar. Aquar. Soc. Toronto*) 5(2): 1-4.

Schneidewind, F. 1999. *Kaiserfische.* Tetra-Verlag, Bissendork-Wulften.

Senou, H. 2001. Records of two introduced angelfishes, *Pomacanthus maculosus* and *Apolemichthys xanthurus* from Japan. *I.O.P. Diving News.* 12:2-5.

Shen, S.C. & C.H. Liu. 1976. Ecological and morphological study of the fish fauna from the waters around Taiwan and its adjacent islands. 17 – A study of sex reversal in a pomacanthid fish *Genicanthus semifasciatus* (Kamohara). *Acta Oceanographica Taiwanica Sci. reports Nat. Taiwan Univ.* No. 6: 140-150.

Shen, S.C. & C.H. Liu. 1979. Clarification of the genera of the angelfishes (family Pomacanthidae). *Acta Oceanographica Taiwanica Sci. reports Nat. Taiwan Univ.* No. 9: 57-77.

Smith, J.L.B. 1949. The fishes of the family Pomacanthidae in the Western Indian Ocean. *Ann. Mag, Nat. Hist.* 12 8: 377-384.

Steene, R.C. 1978. Butterfly and Angelfishes of the World. A.H. & A.W. Reed Pty Ltd., Wellington.

Stratton, R. F. 1992. The Gray Angelfish, *Pomacanthus arcuatus. TFH* 3/92.

Suzuki, K., Hioki, S., Tanaka, Y., & K. Iwasa. 1979. Spawning behavior, eggs, larvae, and sex reversal of two Pomacanthine fishes, *Genicanthus lamarck* and *G. semifasciatus,* in the aquarium. *J. Mar. Sci. Technol.,* Tokai Univ. 12: 149-165.

Takeshita, G.Y. 1976. An angel hybrid. *Marine Aquarist* 7(1):27-35.

Thresher, R.E. 1979. Possible mucophagy by juvenile *Holacanthus tricolor* (Pisces: Pomacanthidae). *Copeia* 1979:160-162.

Thresher, R.E. 1980. *Reef Fish.* Palmetto Publishing. St. Petersburg, FL, USA. 171 pp.

Thresher, R.E. 1982. Courtship and Spawning in the Emperor Angelfish *Pomacanthus imperator,* with comments on reproduction by other pomacanthid fishes. *Mar. Biol.* 70: 149-156.

Thresher, R.E. 1984. *Reproduction in Reef Fishes.* TFH Publications Inc., Neptune City, NJ, 399 pp.

Thresher, R.E. & E.B. Brothers. 1985. Reproductive ecology and biogeography of Indo-West Pacific angelfishes (Pisces: Pomacanthidae). *Evolution* 39(4): 878-887.

Yasuda, F. 1967. Some observations on the color of the young forms of *Chaetodontoplus septentrianalis* (T. & S.). *Sci. Rep. Yokosuka City Mus.* 13: 78-81.

Tuskes, P.M. 1980. Observations on Tropical Atlantic angelfish on the reef and in captivity. *Freshwater and Marine Aquarium* 3(5):7-11, 87-90.

Van Der Elst, R. 1985. *A Guide to the Common Sea Fishes of Southern Africa.* 2nd Edition. C. Struik Publ., Cape Town, 398 pp.

Yoichi, S. and M. Kohda. 1995. Anti-egg predator behaviors of the small angelfish *Centropyge ferrugatus* (Pomacanthidae). *Env. Biol. Fish.* 43:401-405.

Yoichi, S. and M. Kohda. 1997. Harem structure of the protogynous angelfish, *Centropyge ferrugatus* (Pomacanthidae). *Env. Biol. Fish.* 49:333-339

Index

Photography cooperation:
Aquarium Factory Blue Harbor,
Aqua Shop Nagashin, Area, Barrier Reef, B-Box Aquarium,
Bora Bora, Chouousuizokukan, Clown fish, Daiichi Vision,
Earth, El Cube, Hikaru Aquarium,
Kamihata Fish Industry Group, Kaneki Co., ltd,
Penguin Village, Marine Angel, Marine House, Marine Mate,
Marine, Tropical Fish Kuki, Namamugi Kaisugyo Center,
Natural, Natural Marine Club, Nikaai Center, Realize, Rio,
Shellfish, Splash, Tokyo Sun Marine, Tropical & Marine, Wing,
Wish & Honesty, Masahiro Ando, Yoshio Bando,
Bloomberg L.P., Kakinoki, Clinic, Den Aquaroom Shinjuku,
Hiroshi Koumoto, Makoto Matsuoka, Youichi,
Morita, Kinya Oomachi, Nobuyuki Seki,
Hiroyuki Shidara, Masayuki Tamaki, Michiaki Tanaka,
Tomoyuki Urakami, Yoshitou Yanai

Special thanks to: J. Charles Delbeek and Stephen Altit

Contributors of photographs:
John Coppolino, Charles Delbeek,
Naoyuki Hashimoto (Aqualife), Alicia Honn,
Riki Ikeda (Aqualife), Toshiharu Ishibashi (Aqualife),
Osmar Junior, Michinobu Kobayashi, Osamu Morishita,
Tsuneo Nakamura (volvox), Hisayuki Oonuma,
Richard L. Pyle, John E. Randall, Julian Sprung, Takashi Togasi

Translation by Tetsuo Otake
Editing by Julian Sprung
Design and production by Daniel N. Ramirez

You should be able to find this book in your local library,
book store, dive shop, aquarium shop, pet store, or public
aquarium. If you cannot find it locally, please contact:

Two Little Fishies, Inc.
d.b.a Ricordea Publishing
1007 Park Centre Blvd.
Miami Gardens, FL 33169 USA
Tél.: (+01) 305-623-7695
Fax : (+01) 305-623-7697
info@twolittlefishies.com
www.twolittlefishies.com